NEW MERMAIDS

General editors
William C. Carroll: Boston University
Brian Gibbons: University of Münster
Tiffany Stern: University College, Oxford

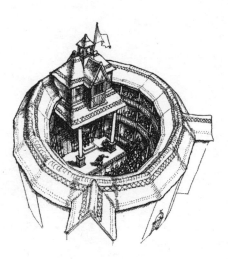

Reconstruction of an Elizabethan Theatre
by C. Walter Hodges

NEW MERMAIDS

THOMAS KYD

THE SPANISH TRAGEDY

edited by J. R. Mulryne

Professor of English
University of Warwick

Methuen Drama • London

New Mermaids

Second edition 1989

3 5 7 9 10 8 6 4

Methuen Drama
A&C Black Publishers Limited
36 Soho Square, London W1D 3QY
www.acblack.com

ISBN: 978 0 7136 6792 9

A CIP catalogue record for this book is
available from the British Library

Printed in the UK by CPI Cox & Wyman, Reading, RG1 8EX

This book is produced using paper that is made from wood grown in
managed, sustainable forests. It is natural, renewable and recyclable.
The logging and manufacturing processes conform to the environmental
regulations of the country of origin.

IN MEMORY OF
T. R. HENN
AND
BRIAN ROTHWELL

CONTENTS

ACKNOWLEDGEMENTS

An editor of *The Spanish Tragedy* owes many debts, especially to earlier editors. I am chiefly indebted to F. S. Boas, whose work forms the basis of modern study of Kyd, and to the indispensable scholarly edition of *The Spanish Tragedy* by Philip Edwards. Professor Edwards put me further in his debt by lending me his photostat copies of the first edition of the play. I am also much indebted to the full study of Kyd by Arthur Freeman. Other debts, of an interpretative and scholarly kind, are acknowledged in the footnotes and in the list of further reading. Like all teachers I have learned a great deal from my students, particularly in the second-year class at the University of Edinburgh. I also have to thank the same University for grants-in-aid towards the research behind this book.

In preparing this revised edition, I am much indebted to my colleague in the Graduate School of Renaissance Studies, University of Warwick, Dr Margaret Shewring, for unstinting practical help, and for her vivid understanding of Elizabethan plays in performance.

J. R. MULRYNE

ABBREVIATIONS

(See also the list of Further Reading, under the authors' surnames.)

1592	the octavo-in-fours edition of *The Spanish Tragedy* printed in that year
1594	the octavo-in-fours of that year
1602	the quarto of that year
Boas	F. S. Boas ed., *Works of Thomas Kyd*, Oxford, 1901
Cairncross	Andrew S. Cairncross ed., *The First Part of Hieronimo* and *The Spanish Tragedy* (Regents Renaissance Drama Series), London, 1967
Edwards	Philip Edwards ed., *The Spanish Tragedy* (The Revels Plays), London, 1959
ELR	*English Literary Renaissance*
JEGP	*Journal of English and Germanic Philology*
JMRS	*Journal of Medieval and Renaissance Studies*
Joseph	Bertram Joseph ed., *The Spanish Tragedy* (The New Mermaids), London, 1964
McIlwraith	A. K. McIlwraith ed., *Five Elizabethan Tragedies* (The World's Classics), Oxford, 1938
MLN	*Modern Language Notes*
MLQ	*Modern Language Quarterly*
MLR	*Modern Language Review*
MRDE	*Medieval and Renaissance Drama in England*
O.E.D.	*The Oxford English Dictionary*
PQ	*Philological Quarterly*
RORD	*Research Opportunities in Renaissance Drama*
RQ	*Renaissance Quarterly*
Schick	J. Schick ed., *The Spanish Tragedy* (The Temple Dramatists), London, 1898
s.d.	stage direction
SEL	*Studies in English Literature*
s.p.	speech prefix
SP	*Studies in Philology*
Tilley	M. P. Tilley, *A Dictionary of the Proverbs in England in the Sixteenth and Seventeenth Centuries*, Ann Arbor, Michigan, 1950

INTRODUCTION

THE AUTHOR

THOMAS KYD belongs to the first generation of Elizabethan playwrights. He was born in 1558, six years before Shakespeare and Marlowe, fifteen years before Jonson, and more than twenty years before Middleton and Webster. His death in 1594, at the age of thirty-six, preceded the staging of almost all the Elizabethan masterpieces, save his own *Spanish Tragedy* and the plays of Marlowe.

Kyd was baptised at the Church of St Mary Woolnoth in London on 6 November 1558, the child of a prosperous middle-class family.[1] His father, Francis Kyd, achieved some distinction as a scrivener, serving as Warden of the Company of Scriveners in 1580. He was a member of an affluent but often disliked profession, with duties in the field of document-copying, and with some importance therefore in the complicated world of Elizabethan law. As a well-educated man, Francis sought a good education for his son, sending Thomas in 1565 at the age of seven to Merchant Taylors' School, a new foundation under the care of Richard Mulcaster, the noted educationalist, whose pupils at this time included Edmund Spenser, Lancelot Andrewes and Thomas Lodge. Here, it seems probable, Kyd became familiar with Latin, French and Italian, and may have had some Greek. Merchant Taylors' may also have first introduced him to the stage, for plays formed part of the boys' training, some even being acted before Queen Elizabeth at Court.

We know virtually nothing of Kyd's early manhood, and can only speculate that he followed his father's profession of scrivener – his handwriting in the few scraps that remain is markedly neat and formal. Certainly he seems not to have attended either university. By 1585, at the age of twenty-seven, he was writing plays for the Queen's Company, the leading London players, though none of his work for this company survives. During 1587–8 he entered the service of a lord, variously identified as Henry, fourth earl of Sussex, or Ferdinando Stanley, Lord Strange, either of whom he may have served as secretary or tutor. His patron was patron also, we know, to a company of players.[2]

---

[1] For full documentation of the known facts about Kyd see Arthur Freeman, *Thomas Kyd: Facts and Problems* (Oxford, 1967)

[2] Freeman argues for the Earl of Sussex; Edwards, p. xx, says the patron was 'possibly' Lord Strange, citing Tucker Brooke and Boas

xi

Information about Kyd's later life comes almost entirely from writings connected with a single incident: his detention and probable torture at the hands of the Privy Council. Details of the affair are in parts uncertain, but it seems that Kyd was arrested during an investigation ordered by the Privy Council on 11 May 1593, to discover the source of certain 'libels'. These were writings directed in all probability against foreigners resident in London. Among Kyd's papers the officers came upon what were described as 'vile heretical Conceiptes denyinge the deity of Jhesus Christe or Savior', and on suspicion of having written blasphemy Kyd was imprisoned.[3] Kyd apparently claimed that the writings were not his but Marlowe's. After Marlowe's death on 30 May 1593, Kyd wrote to Sir John Puckering, asking for release from prison and explaining how Marlowe's papers came to be in his possession. The two authors, he said, were 'wrytinge in one chamber twoe yeares synce' and their papers were shuffled together. He added that Marlowe's known sentiments dovetailed perfectly with those of the 'hereticall Conceiptes'. Both in this letter and in another Kyd amplified the charge; Marlowe is accused, with vivid and sometimes forced illustration, of being blasphemous, disorderly, of treasonous opinions, an irreligious reprobate, 'intemp[er]ate & of a cruel hart'. The morality of the affair has been much disputed, some scholars thinking that Kyd acted disgracefully. He may, however, have suspected that Marlowe informed on him, he may have guessed or known that Marlowe was a spy for Walsingham (and therefore deserved what accusations came his way), or he may in his anxiety to escape prison and torture have slandered his former acquaintance only when he knew he was dead.[4] It is doubtful whether the truth will ever be known. In any case Kyd was himself dead little more than a year later, his death hastened, it seems probable, by his experiences in prison. He was buried at St Mary Colchurch in London on 15 August 1594.

Kyd's writings may well have been much more extensive than those that have come down to us as his. Besides *The Spanish Tragedy* we have on good authority only a translation of Tasso's *Padre di Famiglia* (published in 1588 under the title *The Householder's Philosophy*). Kyd may have written *Soliman and*

---

[3] He may also have had in his possession some of the 'libels' originally complained of. Quotations in this paragraph are from contemporary documents reproduced in Freeman, pp. 26–30. W. D. Briggs (*SP*, 20 (1920), 153–9) has shown the 'conceiptes' are transcripts from an early sixteenth-century theistic treatise, already in print, and scarcely 'atheistic'

[4] Marlowe was in fact arrested (18 May) shortly after Kyd, whether on Kyd's information is not known. He was released on 20 May, ten days only before he was stabbed to death at Deptford

Perseda, a play that shares its main source with Hieronimo's last-act play-within-the-play in *The Spanish Tragedy*; but the evidence is not conclusive. A play known as *I Hieronimo* may, in one form or another, be Kyd's; a kind of fore-piece to *The Spanish Tragedy*, it was perhaps written after the major play, to capitalise on its success. The text we have, published in 1605 by Thomas Pavier, is written in a style rather unlike Kyd's and may derive from a revision of the play by another hand.[5] Notoriously, Kyd may also be the author of an early version of *Hamlet*, now lost. Although the evidence rests, in the first instance, on little more than widely disputed allusions in Thomas Nashe's preface for Robert Greene's *Menaphon*, the balance of probabilities seems to incline towards Kyd's having in fact written such a play. Altogether, the skills apparent in *The Spanish Tragedy*, taken together with early references to Kyd as a dramatist of some note, strongly suggest that much more of his work than now survives found its way on to the sixteenth-century stage.

THE PLAY

Authorship and Date

Until 1773 no editor or dramatic historian attached the name of Thomas Kyd to his one independent surviving play. Early printings carried no author's name. Thomas Heywood, in his *Apology for Actors* (1612), did, however, refer to 'M. Kid, in his Spanish Tragedy', and this attribution was taken up in Thomas Hawkins's *The Origin of the English Drama* (Oxford, 1773). There is no reason to doubt Kyd's authorship.

The date of *The Spanish Tragedy* has long been a matter of dispute. The point is significant to literary historians, for a good deal in their account of the development of English tragedy depends on accurate dating of this play. Arthur Freeman writes:

> If the play precedes *The Jew of Malta* and *The Massacre at Paris* it contains the first Machiavellian villain; if it precedes *John a Kent and John a Cumber* it contains the earliest modern play-within-play; and if it precedes *Titus Andronicus* it may also be styled the first modern revenge tragedy. Given a date before 1587 and *Tamburlaine*, one might incontrovertibly call Kyd's play the first extant modern tragedy, without qualification.[6]

[5] Cairncross thinks Pavier's text a 'memorial reconstruction' of a play by Kyd. His evidence is not convincing
[6] Freeman, pp. 70–1

But despite the attractions of a firm date no scholar has so far
succeeded in establishing one. Certainly the play must have been
written before 23 February 1592, for on that day it was performed
by Lord Strange's men for Henslowe. It was written after 1582,
probably, as it adapts material from Thomas Watson's *Hekatompa-
thia*, entered in the Stationers' Register during that year.[7] But
between these dates all is inference.[8] T. W. Baldwin places the date
as early as 1583–4, while Philip Edwards, John Dover Wilson and
W. W. Greg all prefer a date at the other end of the scale in 1590 or
1591. Boas suggests 1585–7; Tom McAlindon, calling the play
'quite the most important single play in the history of English
drama', places it conjecturally between 1585 and 1590.[9] Arthur
Freeman finds the tone of the Spanish allusions a 'pre-Armada tone'
(because it is 'a trifle shrill' rather than, as it would have been after
the victory, confident or patronising); yet he admits this gives him
only 'a modest excuse for dating the play before 1588'. Eugene Hill,
on the other hand, is inclined to a date 'no earlier than mid-1589',
because of the play's unflattering view of the Portuguese, which
would be appropriate after their failure to rise in support of Drake's
mission to re-establish King Antonio in Lisbon in that year.[10] Philip
Edwards, referring to suggested parallels with *2 Tamburlaine*, *The
Jew of Malta*, *King John*, *3 Henry VI* and Thomas Watson's
Meliboeus, concludes: 'No reader will need to be warned of the
entire absence of proof in these parallels; they are brought forward
none the less, straws as they are, because the date they would hint
at, namely 1590, seems to me not at all inappropriate to the style
and manner of *The Spanish Tragedy*.'[11] In the absence of firmer
evidence we can only place the date somewhere between the outer
limits of 1582 and 1592, with a balance of conjecture in favour of
the later years.

Sources and Background

The Spanish Tragedy is unusual among Elizabethan plays in having

---

[7] Even this is uncertain: Kyd, an acquaintance of Watson's, might have read his
work in manuscript

[8] The fullest discussions of dating come in Edwards, pp. xxi–xxvii and in Freeman,
pp. 70–9; see also Boas, pp. xxviii–xxxi; T. W. Baldwin, 'On the Chronology of
Thomas Kyd's Plays', *MLN*, 40 (1925), 343–9; W. W. Greg, 'The Works of Thomas
Kyd', *MLQ*, 4 (1901), 186–90. J. D. Wilson offers his dating in his edition of *King
John*, pp. liii and 115–16

[9] T. E. McAlindon, *English Renaissance Tragedy* (London, 1986), p. 55

[10] Eugene D. Hill, 'Senecan and Vergilian Perspectives in *The Spanish Tragedy*',
ELR, 15 (1985), p. 154, n. 25

[11] Edwards, p. xxvii. Harold Brooks also favours a late dating; see 'Marlowe and
Early Shakespeare' in *Christopher Marlowe*, ed. Brian Morris (London, 1968), p. 79

no major narrative source. A parallel story, about a young prince, Adilon, and his beloved, Clorinda, appears it is true in Henry Wotton's translation of the tales of Jacques Yver, published in 1578 under the title *A Courtlie Controversie of Cupid's Cautels*. But even if Kyd worked from this tale, he adapted it very freely.[12] He used another of Yver's tales, perhaps at one remove, as the basis for Hieronimo's play-within-the-play in Act IV. The story of Soliman and Perseda may be taken either directly from Yver or from the anonymous play of the same title frequently attributed to Kyd himself.[13] Here again, Kyd adapted freely, altering the story's ending to fit his tragedy.

There are a small number of possible literary sources for a particular incident in the play. The episode of Lorenzo's cunning disposal of Pedringano may draw on the anonymous *A Copie of a Letter* (1584), which tells how the Earl of Leicester rid himself of an unwanted accomplice, a thief called Gates, by affecting to be his protector while actually arranging his death.[14] The incident, one of the most memorable in the play, may have evoked for Elizabethans one or more reference points in classical or later humanistic literature. Frank Ardolino associates the empty box, which Pedringano mistakenly thinks holds his pardon, with the mythical Pandora's box, said to contain all human good and ill, but when opened found to contain hope only. Ardolino interprets the device as showing 'that all earthly action is, in many respects, as delusory and doomed as Pedringano's hope for a pardon'.[15] Barbara Baines prefers to associate the episode with the so-called 'Silenus box', roughly carved and ugly on the outside, but with a beautifully worked figure of a god within. The box, first mentioned in Plato's *Symposium*, became for Erasmus, in *The Praise of Folly* and elsewhere, a favourite symbol for the discrepancy between actuality and right behaviour, appearance and reality, world and stage.[16] Whether either of these is consciously invoked, or directly present to the minds of some or all of Kyd's audience, each is certainly apt to the ironic structures and significances of *The Spanish Tragedy*. Another of the play's episodes, Viluppo's false accusation of

---

[12] For a summary of the tale see Freeman, p. 51

[13] For a discussion of these possibilities see Edwards, p. xlviii

[14] See Edwards, p. xlix

[15] Frank Ardolino, 'The Hangman's Noose and the Empty Box: Kyd's use of dramatic and mythological sources in *The Spanish Tragedy* (III, iv–vii)', *RQ*, 30 (1977), 339. Ardolino explains that the container for the dangerous gifts, originally a jar or vase (in Porphyry two vases), becomes a box in Erasmus, *Adagiorum Chiliades Tres* (1508), the most popular Renaissance version of the myth

[16] Barbara Baines, 'Kyd's Silenus Box and the Limits of Perception', *JMRS*, 10 (1980), 41–51

Alexandro, may draw in a not dissimilar way on a book with a significant place in the humanist tradition, the *Calumny* of Lucian of Samosata. Ronald Broude has shown how Viluppo's tactics in falsely persuading the Viceroy are reminiscent of those used by the figure of the slanderer in Lucian's book.[17]

Study of these sources shows how freely Kyd worked as a playwright, and how responsive his work is to some notable intellectual interests of his day. Each of them applies, however, to one aspect or episode only of *The Spanish Tragedy*. Far more difficult to specify and assess are the pervasive influences, literary, moral and political, which together affect the overall outlook and temper of the play. Something must nevertheless be said about three of these: first, contemporary attitudes to Revenge; second, the Senecan allusions and strategies that characterise the play's tactics and texture (together with their Virgilian antitypes); and third, the politics of England's conflict with Spain in the 1580s, and their bearing on the play's interests.

The topic of Revenge, as explained below, is central to *The Spanish Tragedy*. Michael Hattaway is right to protest against any attempt to explain the play's 'meanings' by quoting from the work of contemporary moral theologians and jurists,[18] yet a sense of the immediately controversial nature of the topic is pertinent to an understanding of the frame of mind in which Kyd's first audiences would respond to the play's action, and to its protagonist, Hieronimo. Elizabethan law specifically forbade vengeance for personal injury, and the Bible ('Vengeance is mine; I will repay, saith the Lord') appeared quite straightforwardly to reserve vengeance to God, not man. Yet contemporary writers, including orthodox theorists, expressed a certain sympathy for private vengeance, at least when the law was unable or unwilling to provide an effective remedy. Even the strict Francis Bacon admitted that 'the most tolerable sort of revenge is for those wrongs which there is no law to punish; else a man's enemy is still before hand, and it is two for one'.[19] *The Spanish Tragedy* needs to be understood within these somewhat contradictory perspectives. Joel Altman has drawn attention to the apparent moral inconsistency of a play that seems to underwrite a quest for vengeance while presenting very vividly, through its hero particularly, the Christian objections to such a quest. But the play, as Altman notes, makes positive use of these

[17] Ronald Broude, 'Time, Truth, and Right in *The Spanish Tragedy*', *SP*, 68 (1971), 130–45, esp. pp. 134–5

[18] Michael Hattaway, *Elizabethan Popular Theatre: Plays in Performance* (London, 1982), p. 104

[19] Quoted Fredson T. Bowers, *Elizabethan Revenge Tragedy* (Princeton, 1940), p. 36

conflicts. Far from being homiletic in intention, its action serves as one of the 'neutral places in which to arouse emotions, ask certain broad philosophical questions, and expound a variety of attitudes towards the tragic story being unfolded'.[20] Our view of Andrea's quest is divided and complex, as is our view of Hieronimo's; and Hieronimo's experience is rendered tragic, as we give and withhold sympathy, not straightforwardly heroic. A crucial preoccupation of the late sixteenth century is thus placed within an ironic double perspective, and our understanding of it made richer.

Kyd's debt to Seneca and to Senecan imitators such as Giraldi Cinthio (1504–73) is a matter both of structure and of expression. The framing device of Andrea's Ghost and the use of the prologue are Senecan in origin, and revenge is a principal Senecan theme. Kyd quotes Seneca directly, makes use of Senecan tags in translation, and owes a general stylistic debt to Senecan rhetoric. His use of stichomythia (answering single lines of verse dialogue) repeats, for example, a Senecan technique.[21] But more significant than the imitation of Senecan style is the recreation in *The Spanish Tragedy* of the emotional and political climate of a Senecan play. Eugene Hill, in an important article, shows how Kyd has appropriated for his own work some of Seneca's typifying interests. A Senecan play, as Hill puts it, conveys 'the texture of evil in a hopelessly corrupt polity'; characteristically, such a play depicts 'the bursting forth of malign forces . . . from the underworld, forces which in the course of the play infest and destroy a royal house.'[22] Kyd's tragedy, that is, represents a genuine *translatio studii*, a work of cultural reclamation that re-makes for sixteenth-century audiences Seneca's horrifying vision of political collapse and personal waste. Moreover, an Elizabethan audience would have been aware of the implicit contrast between Seneca's dismal view of man and society and the optimistic vision expressed in the *Aeneid* of Virgil. The Induction scene of *The Spanish Tragedy* is directly reminiscent of book VI of the *Aeneid*. Its central figure, Andrea, is far, however, from being another Aeneas. Indeed, as Hill points out, Andrea's experience and outlook offer a systematic inversion of those of Aeneas. *Pius* (that is, dutiful) Aeneas becomes, in Kyd's play,

---

[20] Joel B. Altman, *The Tudor Play of Mind: Rhetorical Inquiry and the Development of Elizabethan Drama* (Berkeley and Los Angeles, and London, 1978), p. 269
[21] Discussions of Kyd and the Senecan tradition will be found in T. S. Eliot, 'Seneca in Elizabethan Translation', in *Selected Essays* (London, 1932), pp. 65–108; Bowers, pp. 41–7; F. L. Lucas, *Seneca and Elizabethan Tragedy* (Cambridge, 1922); P. Simpson, 'The Theme of Revenge in Elizabethan Tragedy' in *Studies in Elizabethan Drama* (Oxford, 1955); and in Edwards and Freeman. For direct Senecan reference in the text see notes to this edition at III, xiii, 6, 12–13, 35
[22] Hill, p. 146

proud Andrea; where Aeneas sets out to find his place in the world
of the living, Andrea looks for a position among the dead; Virgil's
Sybil (the guide of Aeneas) is ever alert, while Revenge, Andrea's
mentor, behaves inconsequentially and falls asleep; Aeneas learns
ultimately of the glorious destiny of Rome, Andrea of the
destruction of Spain.[23] Hovering behind the Virgilian allusions
would be, for Elizabethans, the knowledge that England's future
prosperity was becoming associated, in poetry and drama, with the
happy fortunes predicted in the *Aeneid* for Rome. The *Aeneid*
stands, in this regard, as an implicit ironic frame within which the
Senecan landscape of *The Spanish Tragedy* may be viewed.

The Spanish Tragedy was written during the middle or later years
of the 1580s, or the very first years of the 1590s. These were years
of anxiety among Englishmen about the probability of Spanish
invasion, leading to the Armada year of 1588, as well as of anxiety
over the numerous plots, assumed to be Spanish in origin, hatched
against Elizabeth throughout. Protestant polemic of the 1580s
depicted Spain as a place of personal depravity and political
corruption. An influential group within the court pursued a
vigorous anti-Spanish policy both before and after the Armada.[24]
One way for Kyd's first audiences to respond to *The Spanish
Tragedy* was to see the play as showing the merited collapse of a
depraved enemy. Almost at the play's end the King of Spain, as he
observes the carnage on the stage, cries out:

> What age hath ever heard such monstrous deeds?
> My brother, and the whole succeeding hope
> That Spain expected after my decease!   (IV, iv, 202–4)

Contemporaries would see Kyd as having employed the theatrical
idiom of Seneca to enmesh modern Spain in the nightmarish world
of political tragedy. The countervailing Virgilian myth of prosperous destiny is associated with England, at least implicitly, in
Hieronimo's dumb show in Act I, scene iv. There, English warriors
subdue both Spanish and Portuguese enemies. The complacency of
the King of Spain in interpreting these shows would be understood
by English audiences as a mark of Spanish blindness to the role
England was called on to play in world politics.

The political significance of *The Spanish Tragedy* would shade
easily for sixteenth-century audiences into its theological significance. Political success for England and destruction for Spain

[23] Hill, pp. 147–50
[24] See, for example, J. E. Neale, *Queen Elizabeth I* (London, 1934); J. B. Black, *The
Reign of Elizabeth* (second edition, Oxford, 1959); and R. B. Wernham, *The Making
of Elizabethan Foreign Policy* (Berkeley and Los Angeles, 1980)

would be seen not merely as political in character, but as the expression in political terms of the divine management of human affairs. It is possible to interpret the play, as Ronald Broude does, as exemplifying the familiar commonplace *Veritas filia temporis* (truth the daughter of time). The text was a frequent one in anti-Spanish Protestant polemic of the 1580s and 1590s. Time brings *four* truths to birth in the course of *The Spanish Tragedy*: the revealing of innocence as Bel-Imperia is vindicated; the detection of calumny as Alexandro is cleared; the revelation of Horatio's murder; and the bringing to light and punishment of Spanish corruption. It is the last of these which draws together the personal and nationalistic interests of the play. 'The disaster which befalls Kyd's Spain,' Broude writes

> is thus representative of the doom awaiting all nations in which the laws of God are ignored. Viewed in this way, *The Spanish Tragedy* must have offered welcome comfort to Englishmen of the '80s, reassuring them that no matter how precarious their situation might seem, Divine Providence would punish their enemies' wickedness and Time would vindicate the truth and justice of the English cause.[25]

Theme and Structure

In the scene that closes Act III of *The Spanish Tragedy* the Ghost of Andrea rebukes Revenge for neglecting his office. Revenge's answer might serve as gloss on the whole play:

> Thus worldlings ground, what they have dreamed, upon.
> Content thyself, Andrea: though I sleep,
> Yet is my mood soliciting their souls; ...
> Behold, Andrea, for an instance how
> Revenge hath slept, and then imagine thou
> What 'tis to be subject to destiny.   (III, xv, 18–20, 26–8)

All in the play's main action ground their thoughts and deeds on 'dreams'; most are solicited by Revenge's mood; all are subject to destiny. Within the ironic co-ordinates defined by these terms the play's meaning takes shape.

The Spanish Tragedy was written among the first of a group of Elizabethan plays now known as tragedies of Revenge. In an obvious way, the play's action is set in motion and sustained by revenge intrigues: Andrea seeks revenge for his death in battle at the hands of Balthazar: Bel-imperia looks for vengeance for the death of Andrea, her lover; Balthazar and Lorenzo seek revenge on Horatio for winning Bel-imperia's love; Hieronimo pursues ven-

[25] Broude, pp. 144–5

geance for the murder, by Lorenzo and Balthazar, of his son
Horatio. From these intrigues develops all the rest of the play's
narrative; as Philip Edwards writes, '*The Spanish Tragedy* is a play
about the passion for retribution, and vengeance shapes the entire
action.'[26] But quite as remarkable as this dominance of plot is the
range of attitudes that prompt the characters to vengeance: the
slight to Andrea's honour, and the ending of his love plans, that
come with death in battle; the aversion Bel-imperia feels for her
lover's killer; the envy Balthazar cherishes for a successful rival in
love and war; the outrage felt by Hieronimo on the assassination of
his innocent son. Each of these characters is in some sense injured
by one or more of the others, and each seeks to revenge the injury.
Revenge is central to *The Spanish Tragedy*, as to others among the
great Elizabethan plays, because it offers a convenient way of
dramatising human conflict; blood revenge exaggerates, and makes
more dramatic, familiar antagonisms. Criticism of Kyd's play has
sometimes complained that it is structurally weak and morally
unallowable because its initiating and concluding actions centre on
an incident which, in law and even in sentiment, ought not to be
revenged. Andrea was killed, it has been pointed out, in formal if
uneven battle.[27] The tragedy gets under way, it is said, only when
the murder of Horatio provides a more acceptable cause for
revenge. Such criticism is misguided because Kyd's interest lies in
the consequences, proportionate or not, of human enmity. When
the play concludes in the satisfaction of Andrea and Revenge, we
may feel that morally there is a good deal to deplore: the waste and
deaths that feed that satisfaction. But we feel equally the bitter
consistency of motive and action that has led to this point. Kyd has
dramatised, through the revenge idiom, that is to say, a rigorously
coherent and emotionally convincing set of human circumstances
that in the last analysis are tragic, not moralistic, in character.

Seeing the play in this light explains the framework within which
Kyd has placed the main action. Andrea's search for a resting place
in the classical underworld stands for the disappointed man's desire
for satisfaction. Thwarted by death of fulfilment as lover or
'martialist', he is unable to find rest in the underworld. Only when
the goddess Proserpine bids Revenge to sponsor his privileged view
of subsequent events can he achieve rest. The gods in the play are
gods that watch over, and promote or thwart, human desires – or
dreams. Only by circumstance do they become gods of morality
(when we think the desires and their realisation justified); even
more rarely do they come within an acceptable Christian sense of

[26] Edwards, p. li
[27] See I, iv, 21–6 and note

the word God. Almost all the play's major characters appeal at one time or other to Aeacus, Minos, Rhadamanth, Pluto or Proserpine; when they do so they are appealing to the amoral overseers of Fortune. Heaven in this tragedy is normally the province of such gods as these; fittingly, in a play that concerns itself with the working-out of Revenge. Far from offering a complacently Christian-moralistic framework, the play is reminiscent, as Sacvan Bercovitch has noted, of an Empedoclean vision of human destiny, where 'the justice of evil' compels men 'sinfully to pollute [their] ... hands with blood'. Convincingly, he interprets the entire play as an extended version of the grim Empedoclean philosophy of human experience, with love begetting strife and strife love in an unending cycle.[28]

Interpretation of *The Spanish Tragedy* as a revenge play successfully identifies the mainspring of the play's action. It fails, however, on the surface at least, to account for certain of the play's scenes, especially those that take place in Portugal. 'The Portuguese court', writes Philip Edwards, 'could have been introduced more economically and the relevance of theme is very slight.'[29] Studies by Ejner Jensen and G. K. Hunter have tried to demonstrate the pertinence of these and other scenes by displacing the play's focus from revenge to justice. The tragedy's 'chief unifying theme', according to Jensen, 'is not revenge but the problem of justice'; Hunter agrees that 'the play is not centrally concerned with the enactment of revenge. Much more obsessive is the question of justice.'[30] Justice, or judgment, serves indeed as a major preoccupation. Not only is Hieronimo himself a judge but instances of judging and misjudging occur repeatedly. Andrea seeks judgment from Aeacus, Rhadamanth and Minos, and, on their reaching deadlock, from the higher court of Pluto and Proserpine. The King of Spain is called on to arbitrate the rival claims to Balthazar of Lorenzo and Horatio. The Viceroy of Portugal is led into, and then narrowly avoids, a miscarriage of justice in the case of Alexandro and Villuppo. Hieronimo questions the 'justice' of the Heavens, while himself administering justice in others' causes. Pedringano is hanged despite promises to subvert the course of justice. Hieronimo's playlet of *Soliman and Perseda* may be construed as a kind of last judgment, its sentences interpreted by Andrea and confirmed, we expect, by Proserpine. Justice, then, or rather the securing of

[28] Sacvan Bercovitch, 'Love and Strife in Kyd's *Spanish Tragedy*', *SEL*, 9 (1969), p. 226

[29] Edwards, p. liii

[30] Ejner J. Jensen, 'Kyd's *Spanish Tragedy*; The Play Explains Itself', *JEGP*, 64 (1965), 8; Hunter, 'Ironies of Justice in *The Spanish Tragedy*', *Renaissance Drama*, 8 (1965), 92

justice, might be named the play's central interest. But justice and revenge are not really separate issues. In the judgment Andrea seeks they are identical; Revenge sponsors the decisions of Proserpine's court. For Hieronimo the only problem is the straightforward practical one of arranging circumstances so that justice brings about revenge. In other cases, justice, though in danger of mistake, is the simple instrument of vengeance: the Viceroy condemns Alexandro for, as he thinks, the murder of his son; Pedringano is condemned and executed for the killing of Serberine. When Lorenzo and Balthazar die, Hieronimo's vengeance serves in place of the justice they have till then averted. Sometimes, as in the King's arbitration or in Hieronimo's promises to the suitors, justice is a matter of 'fair play', a situation that falls between justice as retribution and justice in the emotionally loaded sense that Andrea, Bel-imperia and sometimes Hieronimo mean the word. When Hieronimo protests the seeming absence of Heavenly justice, he is protesting certainly the failure of human courts to bring to justice his son's murderers. But he is really talking about a far larger issue, and one that becomes a leading preoccupation of dramatists like Shakespeare and Webster:

> Yet still tormented is my tortured soul
> With broken sighs and restless passions,
> That winged mount, and hovering in the air,
> Beat at the windows of the brightest heavens,
> Soliciting for justice and revenge;
> But they are placed in those empyreal heights,
> Where, counter-mured with walls of diamond,
> I find the place impregnable; and they
> Resist my woes, and give my words no way.   (III, vii, 10–18)

The bafflement of the individual before the ways of Heaven (or Fortune) becomes more embittered in plays later than this. Here the justice Hieronimo seeks is one that operates (as line 14 suggests) through revenge, and the whole play ministers to their eventual triumph. In *The Spanish Tragedy* justice and revenge interact, support and contradict one another in an intricate mirroring of human conflict. In the end, Heaven, it appears, is not deaf, though the Heaven that listens can hardly in human terms be called just. The play enacts, as noted above, the vindication of the saying that truth is the daughter of time; but the unmaskings that occur bring with them much that causes pain, and much that seems in the event unjust.

Kyd's play is held together by instances of judging that finally contribute to the success of revenge; or, in the case of the Portuguese scenes and those that deal with Pedringano, that shadow

revenge's ultimate triumph. But judging is by no means always done
in full knowledge of the facts. On the contrary, *The Spanish
Tragedy* is remarkable for the extent to which Kyd exploits the
ignorance of the characters for ironic effect.[31] By virtue of the
framing action in particular, we in the audience enjoy knowledge
hidden from participants in the main play. We know that the play's
outcome will be disastrous for anyone who opposes Andrea's
revenge, even though the path to vengeance may be tortuous and
revenge delayed. Andrea's doubts and Revenge's reassurance (in
the scenes that close Acts I, II and III), as well as their continued
presence as spectators, merely dramatise overtly the relationship
the audience adopts to the events on stage. We are held between
frustration and detachment as the plot moves forward: frustrated,
like Andrea, that Horatio is killed, Bel-imperia sequestered and
Hieronimo thwarted, but detached, like Revenge, because we know
that Andrea's cause, under his sponsorship, must eventually win
through. The effect of this is to place us in an ironic relationship
with almost everything that happens: all action takes place within a
determined framework to which we, but not the actors, hold the
key. We feel in Act I, scene i, for instance, the threat of oncoming
disaster behind the boastful self-confidence and military display of
the Spanish court, even if we cannot exactly predict the catastrophe
that at the play's end destroys the whole Spanish succession. When
the Spanish King overweeningly exclaims

Then blest be heaven, and guider of the heavens,
From whose fair influence such justice flows   (I, ii, 10–11)

we recognise that heavenly justice may not be as simple or, for him,
as comprehensible as he thinks: the battle he gives such easy thanks
for is the battle of Andrea's death. Equally, we sense behind each
action Balthazar takes, or Lorenzo or Bel-imperia or Hieronimo, the
long shadow of Andrea's revenge, sometimes aiding, sometimes
threatening. Moreover, besides such general ironies as these Kyd
cultivates more particular and overt ironic moments. As Horatio
courts Bel-imperia in Act II, scene ii, for instance, we know that
Pedringano has already betrayed their love; while the two lovers
confess their affection and anticipate love's pleasures the hidden
Balthazar and Lorenzo contradict all they say: the intricate
structure of statement and counterstatement functions like a grim
inversion of the overhearing scenes of comedy. When in a later
scene (II, iv) they invoke night and darkness to countenance their
love-making we scarcely need the sombre if crude irony of
Horatio's

O stay a while and I will die with thee   (II, iv, 48)

[31] See Hunter for a penetrating analysis of this aspect of the play

to underline the equivocal sense in which we have been observing the whole episode. Ironies can run in a contrary direction too, most complexly perhaps in the Portuguese scenes (I, iii and III, i). There we see the Viceroy mourning, while we know his son is in fact alive; and yet the mourning is pertinent also, for we know the son's life is threatened inevitably by Andrea. When the mourning turns to joy in a later scene we appreciate that under the superficial cause of joy lie causes of dread: for by now the Viceroy's son has committed the murder of another son, Horatio, a crime which must inevitably lead to his own destruction. Ironies multiply elsewhere; we are always conscious of the ignorance, sometimes greater, sometimes less, of the characters. Each of them attempts to clear a little space for himself, to impose his will a little, without being able to escape the pattern of consequence established by Revenge. Even the intriguers, the Machiavels, like Lorenzo and his shadow Villuppo, are only attempting, in their own bad way, to control the movements of Fortune. Villuppo is cheated by the merest coincidence: the Ambassador returns from Spain moments before Alexandro is to be executed; Lorenzo's schemes, at first successful, are ultimately defeated by Hieronimo's persistence and Bel-imperia's, and by the operations of chance. Hieronimo is himself another intriguer, a wily revenger forced by circumstances to act unlawfully; an intriguer favoured, however, by the prevailing Fate, as Bel-imperia's letter and then Pedringano's lead him to successful action. Kyd provides us with an emblematic, near-burlesque statement of the whole situation: Pedringano jesting with death (or Fate) as the boy points to the box – empty, despite Pedringano's confidence that it contains his pardon. Each of the play's characters is as vulnerable to an engrossing Fate as Pedringano; and almost all are as blithely unaware as he that they lack the power to turn that Fate aside, whether their purposes are good or ill. The experience of watching *The Spanish Tragedy* is the ironic one of seeing 'truth' gradually vindicated over the ignorance or devising of the characters, whether it is vindicated in the matter of Villuppo, or the death of Serberine, or the main-plot killing of Horatio.

To present his theme Kyd has structured the play masterfully. Not only are the ironies brilliantly cultivated, but episodes are contrived with striking skill to reflect and balance each other. Michael Hattaway has shown, indeed, how the play's strong dramatic rhythm derives from what he calls the architectonic arrangement of *figurae*, consciously placed in key situations throughout.[32] The Viceroy's mourning for his son anticipates and extends Hieronimo's mourning; both weep the death of a son and

[32] Hattaway, p. 106

blame Fortune. Andrea's revenge, the Viceroy's revenge on
Alexandro or Villuppo, Lorenzo's witty disposal of Pedringano,
Hieronimo's revenge for his son – these serve like angled mirrors to
reiterate but never exactly repeat parallel concerns and situations.
Alexandro, the Viceroy, Isabella, Bel-imperia, Hieronimo, Pedringano all see themselves at one time or another as the victim of an
oppressive Fate, and each in a different way tries to rationalise the
position; the author's devising hand has so contrived the action that
we discover a whole range of linked but dissimilar attitudes. To
keep the plot firm, Kyd has arranged that Horatio becomes quite
explicitly a second Andrea (I, iv, 58ff.); he may even (the evidence
is not quite conclusive) make use of a convenient hand-prop to
connect visually the two revenges: the scarf Bel-imperia gave
Andrea to wear in battle was taken from his dead body by Horatio
and offered by Bel-imperia for her new lover to wear; it may be the
same 'bloody handkercher' that Hieronimo takes from his dead
son's body and keeps to the end as revenge token. A contrivance
equally deft operates *within* scenes and episodes: Wolfgang Clemen
has shown how scene after scene observes carefully planned, almost
geometrical patterning, a structural cunning that reflects on the
level of plot the rhetorical niceties of the characters' language.[33] Act
II, scene i, for instance, is structured around Balthazar's twin
speeches, at beginning and end, about Bel-imperia and Horatio;
'thus the two goals of Balthazar's future endeavours are brought
into sharp relief, not only in dialogue enlivened by action, but also
through the rhetorical emphasis of the set speeches'.[34] So too Kyd
has shown he knows how to use stage action to underline the
symmetries of the plot: Balthazar, for instance, first enters with
Lorenzo and Horatio on either side, each laying claim to being his
captor, and thus predicting the dissensions the whole play is about
to elaborate. Even the two plays-within-the-play reflect and echo
each other: the first, the masque of peace in Act I, scene iv, though
counselling humility, is written in honour of Spain's military glory;
the second, the play of Soliman and Perseda, contrives the
destruction of the royal house. And this second play itself provides
perhaps the best example of Kyd's structural cunning, as it reflects
and interprets the tragedy's central theme. There is an intricately
devised appropriateness in the distribution of roles. As Sacvan
Bercovitch explains, Balthazar (as Soliman) and Bel-imperia (as
Perseda) play out their actual tragedies: Soliman, like Balthazar, is
slain by his beloved, and Perseda, like Bel-imperia, is the mistress

[33] Clemen, *English Tragedy before Shakespeare* (London, 1961), esp. pp. 100–12
and 267–77
[34] Clemen, p. 102

who turns murderess. Hieronimo and Lorenzo each adopt another's role, and yet each ironically plays out his own fate: Hieronimo, now turned intriguer, plays the Bashaw who, as Soliman's friend, recalls the Machiavellian Lorenzo; Lorenzo himself, as Erasto, is Perseda's murdered lover, thus shadowing Horatio; and he is killed by Horatio's avengers.[35] More telling still is the episode's general significance. There has been disagreement about whether the 'sundry languages' of the polyglot play were ever spoken on stage; but there can be little disagreement over the almost surreal fashion in which the action of the inset play – death stealing in unperceived amidst a Babel-like confusion of tongues – represents a major idiom of the whole tragedy.[36] Carole Kay finds the detachment of words from their anchorage in reality a disturbingly prominent feature of Kyd's treatment of the main play's events. There are, she notes, five separate and variant descriptions of the death of Andrea.[37] So, too, *Soliman and Perseda* is, at the verbal level, confusingly beyond interpretation. But the inset play also reflects the variance between detached, 'aesthetic' pleasure and real suffering that characterises the tragedy as a whole. The two audiences for this final play, Andrea and Revenge on the one hand, the Spanish and Portuguese courts on the other, understand the show quite differently, the first with detachment, the second with a growing realisation of the reality of what they are seeing. So too, in the tragedy at large, Revenge and Andrea take pleasure in the working-out of a scheme of events which for participants in the play brings suffering and death.[38] The parallels are enhanced and completed in both cases by the perceptions of a real-life audience in the sixteenth-century or twentieth-century theatre. These perceptions include and go beyond those of participants in the drama, and like theirs brace aesthetic enjoyment against pain, and detachment against empathy. By structural cunning such as this, Kyd makes his play live as an image of the contradictory impulses of theatre, which are arguably those of lived experience itself.

As a result of all these features, *The Spanish Tragedy* emerges as a dark tragedy indeed, with the pain of the experience mitigated

---

[35] See Bercovitch, pp. 224–5

[36] For an elaborate discussion of this point see S. F. Johnson, '*The Spanish Tragedy* or Babylon Revisited', in *Essays on Shakespeare and Elizabethan Drama*, ed. Richard Hosley (London, 1963)

[37] Carole McGinnis Kay, 'Deception through Words: a reading of *The Spanish Tragedy*', *SP*, 74 (1977), 20–38, *passim*

[38] See Barry B. Adams, 'The Audiences of *The Spanish Tragedy*', *JEGP*, 68 (1969), 221–36. Adams notes also that the masque of Act I, scene iv introduces the 'real life' of the Earls of Gloucester and Kent, and of John of Gaunt, into a fictionalised situation, thus predicting and contrasting with the inset play of *Soliman and Perseda*

only by the theatrical devices that allow us to maintain a distance as we view. Donna B. Hamilton has drawn attention to the almost Beckett-like irony of the play's last line, as spoken by Revenge:[39]

I'll there begin their endless tragedy.

The play's landscape of suffering begins again where it ends, with Revenge, the play's figure for disorder and destruction in human affairs, still the presiding divinity. The only outcome of all the efforts of the play's people – good and bad and simple victims – to establish order and justice appears to be a further cycle of pain.

Characterisation and Language

In recent writing on *The Spanish Tragedy*, there has been a tendency to admire the play's structural deftness, while neglecting its power of character creation, and its strong dramatic language. It is a mistake to deflect attention, however, from Kyd's invention of playable roles, and particularly from the role of Hieronimo. Hieronimo is the play's centre because he tries more persistently and with more emotion than anyone else, within the limits imposed by this play, to find the truth and establish justice – though of a crude kind. In so doing he draws an audience's sympathy and involvement, despite arguments, now largely abandoned by critics, that he forfeits our respect when he begins to act unlawfully.[40] Hieronimo engages our interest as the beleaguered man who tries in all honesty, and with outstanding pertinacity, to set right the wrongs of his time. In this he of course anticipates Hamlet, the character with whom he has notoriously been linked by dramatic historians. It is true that for Hieronimo the world is not as question-fraught as it is for Shakespeare's hero, largely because Kyd scarcely allows Hieronimo to question his own nature and motives, nor is he skilled enough to make the environment within which Hieronimo acts anything like so disturbingly equivocal as the world of *Hamlet*. Yet the seeds of self-questioning are there (the soliloquy that begins Act III, scene xii, e.g., anticipates Hamlet's musings on suicide), and so are the first signs of a difficult, it not quite an equivocal world: the intrigues of Lorenzo, the hints of a double standard for judging strong and weak, the business-preoccupied mentality that thwarts justice and revenge in the latter part of Act III, scene xii. If Hieronimo is by no means so complex and fascinating a character as

---

[39] Donna B. Hamilton, '*The Spanish Tragedy*: a speaking picture', *ELR*, 4 (1974), 203–17. See the essay *passim* for a challenging account of Kyd's play

[40] For the argument on this point see John D. Ratliff, 'Hieronimo Explains Himself', *SP*, 54 (1957), 112–18

Hamlet, he does share many of the same challenges, and he does pursue his similar quest with comparable unwillingness to prevaricate or compromise, except on the surface. And unlike Hamlet he raises an issue very fruitful for tragedies written later in the Elizabethan decades: his anguished sense that Heaven itself is deaf:

> Where shall I run to breathe abroad my woes,
> My woes whose weight hath wearied the earth?
> Or mine exclaims, that have surcharged the air
> With ceaseless plaints for my deceased son? . . .   (III, vii, 1ff.)

Hieronimo's quest soon slips into less demanding matters of tactics and practicality, but here at least (the whole speech makes the point) Kyd succeeds in writing a poetry of the theatre that fully conveys Hieronimo's sense of a world wholly occupied by his new grief – a grief made more intense because at this stage he cannot summon a comforting belief that a supernatural order oversees his experience or will in any way alleviate his pain.

It is true that even a sympathetic critic will discover moments in this speech of over-emphasis and cliché; and what is true here is true *a fortiori* of other among Hieronimo's soliloquies. A modern reader finds it difficult to adjust to the larger-than-life emphasis, as well as the self-conscious artificiality of structure, in Kyd's stage rhetoric. Profound emotion wedded to exceptional artifice of structure appears to us contradiction and insincerity; we feel more comfortable with those parodies of Hieronimo's speeches that Elizabethan authors soon began to invent. Yet we miss the point of Kyd's dramatic skill if we do not see how subtly he has calculated, in the quoted speech, the alliterative patterns – not so emphatic as to call undue attention to themselves, but strong enough to offer the actor some purchase for moulding the speech-pattern; or if we do not see how naturally, and yet with seeming inevitability, he has controlled the tempo of the speech – an actor will note particularly the way in which exclamation is reined in at the natural pauses of lines 9, 14 and 18. Kyd's strengths as a writer of dramatic verse are at their most remarkable in this and other of Hieronimo's soliloquies. Even the notorious 'O eyes, no eyes' soliloquy (III, ii, 1–52), the most formally patterned and among the most emotional of all Hieronimo's speeches, need not prove impossibly difficult on the modern stage.[41] Kyd's instinct for dramatic speech ensures that here too the cadences of his rhetoric can be turned to account: the rise and fall of emotional intensity, and the implied rhythm of individual sentences, never forget the actor's needs: they provide

---

[41] The speech is fully and perceptively analysed in Clemen, pp. 270–5

opportunities rather for virtuosity. And Kyd can be affectingly
simple where simplicity is in place:

> Ay, now I know thee, now thou nam'st thy son;
> Thou art the lively image of my grief:
> Within thy face my sorrows I may see.
> Thy eyes are gummed with tears, thy cheeks are wan,
> Thy forehead troubled, and thy muttering lips
> Murmur sad words abruptly broken off
> By force of windy sighs thy spirit breathes;
> And all this sorrow riseth for thy son:
> And selfsame sorrow feel I for my son.   (III, xiii, 161–9)

Bazulto as the emblem, the 'lively image', of Hieronimo's sorrow
may appear a somewhat literary device, part of that self-conscious
patterning that spans the whole tragedy. But Hieronimo's meeting
with him provides an opportunity for the expression of genuine
emotion, and Kyd shows that he possesses the theatrical tact to take
advantage of it. The character of Hieronimo, and especially his
soliloquies, provide the growth-points for a whole generation of
tragic heroes and of tragic verse.

To speak of Hieronimo as a fully realised character is perhaps to
misrepresent Kyd's play. *The Spanish Tragedy* stands at the
turning-point between a drama of statement and a drama of
experience (or exploration), and Hieronimo remains largely a
typical rather than an individual figure: the lamenting father, and
wily avenger. Characterisation of the other persons is both slighter
emotionally and, in one or two cases, more obviously helpful to the
actor. The Spanish king and the viceroy of Portugal, it is true,
remain figureheads; Isabella utters a few speeches of lament and
protest without becoming much more than a mouthpiece for lament
and protest. Bel-imperia, on the contrary, comes over as a woman
with definite characteristics. Consider, for example, how freely her
personality emerges from Kyd's masterly re-handling of the
Senecan device of stichomythia (line-by-line dialogue), a device
utterly dead in the hands of earlier and contemporary playwrights:

LORENZO
> Sister, what means this melancholy walk?

BEL-IMPERIA
> That for a while I wish no company.

LORENZO
> But here the prince is come to visit you.

BEL-IMPERIA
> That argues that he lives in liberty.

BALTHAZAR
> No madam, but in pleasing servitude.

BEL-IMPERIA
> Your prison then belike is your conceit.   (I, iv, 77–82)

xxx   INTRODUCTION

The excellence of this does not lie in any of the elaborate verbal schemes we normally associate with Kyd, but in a sparseness that gives the actor ample opportunity. Bel-imperia's icy reserve, her barely veiled hatred of Balthazar, come across sharply in the stilted, glacially polite exchange. Her formidable qualities emerge more clearly as she confronts Lorenzo and Balthazar after her release from imprisonment (III, x, 24ff.); her protests are only less vigorous than the sardonic double-talk she offers in pretended acceptance of their explanations. No actress need have difficulty in playing Bel-imperia as a strong-willed – and sensually incli- ned – woman. The double values of her name, beautiful and domineering, are borne out in her character. Lorenzo, important as the first (certainly among the first) of a line of stage-Machiavels who exploited the Elizabethan delight in cunning, nevertheless remains a more conventional character than his sister. Yet he too is a distinctly playable figure, astute, self-willed and slippery. Tom McAlindon draws attention to the contrasting elements in his nature, calling him 'the man of very gentle birth whose smooth courtliness and jovial affability obscure the fact that he can be compared to a "savage monster, not of human kind" (II, v, 19)'. His companion, Balthazar, is more thoroughly characterised, a rather ineffectual young man, deeply conscious (see II, i, 118–33) of his inferiority to Horatio. And his feelings of inferiority register themselves in his language; as Clemen has pointed out, his repetitive style of speech and his tedious dependence on rhetorical figures are 'exactly in keeping with the irresolute, dependent, puppet-like role' he fills.[42] His opponent, Horatio, suffers from being the ideal young man, perfectly adapted to becoming the victim of a horrid murder; yet while he lives he does at least engage with Bel-imperia in sufficiently vigorous, and sufficiently sex-conscious, dialogue to show that he is no prig. And his love poetry is, at the lowest, better than Balthazar's. The other figures in the tragedy are largely supporting cast without developed characterisa-tion.

The Play on the Stage

The Spanish Tragedy proved on its first appearance an overwhelm-ingly successful stage play. Jean Fuzier's analysis of evidence in the *Diary* of the theatrical entrepreneur Philip Henslowe shows that in the years between early 1592 and late 1597 it was performed under Henslowe's auspices twenty-nine times, a popularity rating only just behind *The Jew of Malta* (thirty-six times) and the lost

[42] McAlindon, p. 60; and Clemen, p. 277

play *The Wise Man of West Chester* (thirty-two times). In that span
of years *The Spanish Tragedy* seems to have been even more in
demand than Marlowe's great tragedy *Dr Faustus*.[43] The play had
been in performance, possibly, even before it is recorded by
Henslowe in 1592. Subsequent years saw it staged by perhaps no
fewer than four of the Elizabethan acting companies (up to 1604):
Strange's Men (in 1592 London's premier company), the Admiral's
Men, Pembroke's Men and, possibly, the Chamberlain's Men
(eventually the King's Men). It was performed at several of
London's theatres: The Rose and The Fortune, certainly, and
possibly The Theatre, The Cross Keys Inn, Newington Butts, The
Curtain and the first Globe.[44] Additions were paid for in 1602, and
other adaptations may well have been commissioned.[45] The play
enjoyed the mocking tribute of parody in, for example, Beaumont's
The Knight of the Burning Pestle, first performed in 1607, a sure
sign of its continued popularity. Claude Dundrap has enumerated
111 allusions to the play by Kyd's contemporaries and successors.[46]
It was reprinted at least nine times before 1633, thus making it
easily available to acting companies outside the main London
theatres, and it may well have been performed right up to the
cessation of playing in 1642. All this testifies to the vitality of Kyd's
theatrical writing and its popular appeal in the late sixteenth and
early seventeenth centuries.

Kyd's theatrical manner is not one which commended itself to
performers of the Restoration or eighteenth-century stage, or to the
professional stage almost to the present. Michael Hattaway has
shown convincingly how the 'strong dramatic rhythm' of Kyd's play
is 'dependent for its effect on the bold architectural symmetry of its
dramatic form' and how its repeated situations (or 'gests') are based
not on the transcription of reality but on 'analogy, on the creation of
figurae, and the architectonic arrangement of these'.[47] In theatres
that were increasingly occupied with psychological realism, and
with social interaction, Kyd's characters and dramatic structures
came rapidly to seem out of date and clumsy. Until the years after

[43] Performed twenty-five times. See Jean Fuzier's 'Carrière et popularité de la
Tragédie Espagnole en Angleterre' in *Dramaturgie et Société*, ed. Jean Jacquot
(1968), 2, 589–606. See also Carol Chillington Rutter, ed., *Documents of the Rose
Playhouse* (Manchester, 1984), p. 24 and Neil Carson, *A Companion to Henlowe's
Diary* (Cambridge, 1988), s.v. *Jeronimo*
[44] See D. F. Rowan, 'The Staging of *The Spanish Tragedy*', in *The Elizabethan
Theatre V*, ed. G. R. Hibbard (London, 1975), pp. 112–23
[45] See 'The "Additions"' below
[46] Claude Dundrap, 'La *Tragédie Espagnole* face à la Critique Elizabéthaine et
Jacobéene', in *Dramaturgie et Sociéte*, 2, 607–31, cited in Rowan, p. 113
[47] Hattaway, p. 106

1970, when English professional theatre was once again presenting unfamiliar classics, *The Spanish Tragedy* remained neglected. Three professional productions since that date, however – at the Mercury Theatre, London (opening 24 September 1973), at the Citizens' Theatre, Glasgow (opening 27 October 1978) and at the National Theatre, London (opening 22 September 1982) – have in their differing ways demonstrated the continuing theatrical vitality latent in Kyd's script.[48]

Realisation of a classic play on the modern stage requires a complex process of rediscovery.[49] Robert David MacDonald's Glasgow production sought to identify the play's outrageous strengths (in Tony Howard's phrase)[50] by considerable adaptation, including the incorporation of material from Kyd's own *The First Part of Hieronimo*. MacDonald employed a physical sensationalism and an inconsequent narrative structure, reminiscent of the theatre of the absurd, in an attempt to find modern equivalents for the cruelty that, judging from the early performance record, appealed so powerfully to sixteenth-century audiences. MacDonald's actors rediscovered too, after initial uncertainty, the rhetorical force of Kyd's language, giving the verse a 'full-voiced and thrilling' delivery.[51] There was less competence, vocally, among the actors of the National Theatre production. Michael Bogdanov's direction and Chris Dyer's strongly focused design, however, 'revealed the tragedy's stern unity and Kyd's firm use of space'.[52] There was significant economy in the devices used. A single stage unit, centrally placed, did duty for all the executions; the figure of Revenge manipulated every detail of the action by giving letters or weapons to the participants; and the corpse of Horatio was finally discovered within a huge wooden image of Revenge, hooded and bearing daggers. Nicholas de Jongh, who thought Bogdanov was right in taking 'the play's surfeit of cruelty and its elongated moans in all seriousness', nevertheless objected to what he took to be 'the ponderous, faked grandeur of the verse, not to mention its metrical lethargy'. He also thought 'the play's marvellous final scene' was

---

[48] For a listing of these and amateur performances of *The Spanish Tragedy* since 1921 (when the play was given an amateur production at Birkbeck College, University of London), see Lisa Cronin, 'A Checklist of Productions in the British Isles since 1880 of Plays by Tudor and Early Stuart Dramatists (excluding Shakespeare)', Supplement 7, *Renaissance Drama Newsletter* (Warwick, 1987)

[49] Detailed discussion of the problems inherent in this process is offered in Jonathan Miller, *Subsequent Performances* (London, 1986), *passim*

[50] Tony Howard, 'Renaissance Drama Productions', *RORD*, 21 (1978), 64–5

[51] Ibid.

[52] Tony Howard, 'Renaissance Drama Productions', *RORD*, 26 (1983), 76–7

'not allowed to become a liberating climactic'.[53] My own recollection endorses Tony Howard's vivid description of the tense and powerful theatricality of the play's last moments, mingling anguish with comic detachment:

> *Soliman and Perseda* was given in 'sundry languages' [in contrast to the English of the Glasgow production], to the embarrassment of the performers and the bewilderment of both the real and fictional audiences (the Court sat close to the 20th-century audience in the lower side balconies). The courtiers were quite blind and clapped everything, especially the coup of Horatio's discovery, and they did not completely understand that the show was a reality until Hieronimo's tongue slapped onto the floor. Trickles, spurts, and finally showers of stage blood added to the chaos (even reaching the front row of the paying public) in which black comedy and horror were inextricable. The National Theatre [audience] seemed astonished by the excess and roared when Revenge promised an even ghastlier 'lasting tragedy' in Hades.[54]

For that twentieth-century audience a partial rediscovery, at least, of the theatrical power known to the early audiences had been effected. It is possible to hope that after centuries of neglect *The Spanish Tragedy* will once again be recognised as a theatre piece of extraordinary force, and be given its due place as a text for frequent exploration on stage.

THE 'ADDITIONS'

The so-called 'Additions' to *The Spanish Tragedy* are grouped at the end of the present text. First printed in 1602 and there incorporated into the original text of the play, they comprise in all some 320 lines. Of the five additional passages, the first, second and fifth are brief and of slight importance, and the fourth is the well-known Painter scene, which amplifies in a striking manner the theme of Hieronimo's grief, and provides a remarkable opportunity for an actor to portray madness. Despite the excellence of some of the writing, however, there can be little doubt that inclusion of these scenes in an acting version would have the effect of upsetting the rhythm of Kyd's play.

It is most unlikely in fact that the 1602 text, including the 'Additions', was ever performed in its existing state. It is, for one thing, exceptionally long. It is more likely that the additional passages were intended to replace parts of Kyd's text which were

[53] Nicholas de Jongh, '*The Spanish Tragedy* at the Cottesloe', *Plays and Players*, Issue No. 351 (December 1982), pp. 24–5
[54] Howard, *RORD*, 26, p. 77

felt by 1602 to be either old-fashioned or weak. Pavier, the publisher of this new edition, may have received from the theatre, or from some intermediary, authorised or not, portions of the new copy; he would then incorporate them as best he could into an example of *1592*. Some support for this theory comes from the rough, or at the least 'free', state of the verse in the additional passages; we may suspect that some kind of printer's bungling has taken place.

The author of the 'Additions' is unknown. Ben Jonson was, we know, paid for revisions to *The Spanish Tragedy*, but those we have are rather unlike his characteristic work, and there are problems (of dating mainly) about connecting Henslowe's payment to Jonson with the printing of *1602*. Jonson certainly may have adapted his style to suit the play he was revising; but equally plausible is the suggestion that the lines are the work of another author, and that Jonson's revision of the play has unfortunately never been printed. Webster, Shakespeare and Dekker are among writers suggested as alternative authors, but the case for any one of them, or for other contemporaries, is not a strong one.

NOTE ON THE TEXT

The 1592 edition of *The Spanish Tragedy* is undated; it has been accepted as an octavo-in-fours of that year on the evidence of a dispute over the ownership of copyright. The dispute was settled by the Stationers' Company on 18 December 1592, when the publisher of *1592*, Edward White, was fined by the Company for 'having printed the spanishe tragedie belonging to Abell Ieffes'. There seems little doubt that printing took place earlier the same year.

1592 is the sole authoritative text of the play, and has of course been used as the basis of the present edition. The 'Additions' were first produced in quarto in 1602, a printing which serves as copy-text for the 'Additions' as given here. Other early editions, printed in 1594, 1599, 1603, 1610, 1615, 1618, 1623, and 1633, will testify to the play's enormous and long-lived popularity. Modern editions include those by Boas (*Works of Thomas Kyd*, 1901), McIlwraith (in *Five Elizabethan Tragedies*, 1938), Schick (The Temple Dramatists, 1898), Edwards (The Revels Plays, 1959), Joseph (The New Mermaids, 1964), Cairncross (Regents Renaissance Drama Series, 1967), and Ross (The Fountainwell Drama Texts, 1968).

All of these have been used in the preparation of the present edition, but the text has been established and checked by a fresh consideration of the British Museum copies of *1592* and *1602*.

Philip Edwards has argued, ingeniously and for the most part persuasively, that copy for *1592* included material of two distinct kinds, one taking the play as far as Act III, scene xiv, the other affecting the remaining scenes. Over the first section the text is a good one, showing little corruption and presenting few problems to the editor; the latter section contains some limited areas of corruption, irregularity and inconsistency. Writing of this second section, Edwards (p. xl) argues that 'the inconsistency in the action, which relates to the play-within-the-play and to Hieronimo's behaviour just before his death, may suggest that the text contains elements of a revised and abridged version of the play'; he adds that the 'presence of one unusually corrupt scene (III, xv) may suggest the use of inferior copy' and postulates that this may be drawn from a now lost edition of the play containing an unauthorised and corrupt version of Kyd's text. Edwards's reasoning explains more convincingly than any other the noticeable difference between the early and late parts of the text, and helps to account for the difficulties attaching to presentation of the last scenes of the play. In general, however, it is clear that *1592* derives from material of high authority, probably Kyd's own manuscript, and not a manuscript originating in the theatre, or one much altered or marked up by theatre officials. In these circumstances, an editor will take care not to alter substantive readings in his copy-text without clear evidence of corruption.

In accordance with the policy of this series, departures from the copy-text in substantive readings are noted among the notes at the foot of the page; earlier editors, whether Elizabethan or more recent, are not acknowledged in these notes except under the general designation 'ed.' In matters of punctuation I have been guided by what I have taken to be the convenience of a modern reader, and by the wish to present a text an actor could readily use on stage. I have therefore lightened somewhat the punctuation of the original (which proved rather formal) by removing commas, by reducing colons to commas, and by excising a fairly large number of unnecessary full stops. When meaning seemed obscure, however, and not just deliberately ambiguous, I have occasionally added punctuation in the hope of assisting a modern reader. When foreign languages are quoted I have, like other recent editors, produced a form of the language recognisable by present-day linguists, though there is no certainty that Kyd originally got these languages 'right' by modern standards. In the matter of explanatory notes I have erred on the side of generosity, especially in providing brief glosses;

I recognise it is irritating to meet glosses one does not need, but it is infinitely more annoying to find an editor has assumed knowledge where none exists. The reader will see that I have been especially persistent in glossing classical allusions. Speech prefixes and the names in stage directions have been modernised and regularised throughout.

FURTHER READING

Adams, Barry B., 'The Audiences of *The Spanish Tragedy*', *JEGP*, 68 (1969), 221–36

Altman, Joel B., *The Tudor Play of Mind: rhetorical inquiry and the development of Elizabethan drama* (Berkeley and Los Angeles, and London, 1978), ch. 9

Ardolino, Frank R., *Thomas Kyd's Mystery Play: myth and ritual in 'The Spanish Tragedy'*, (New York, Berne, Frankfurt am Main, 1985)
    '"In Paris? Mass, and Well Remembered": Kyd's *The Spanish Tragedy* and the English Reaction to the St Bartholomew's Day Massacre', *The Sixteenth Century Journal*, 21 (1990), 481–89

Baines, Barbara J., 'Kyd's Silenus Box and the Limits of Perception', *JMRS*, 10 (1980), 41–51

Barish, Jonas A., '*The Spanish Tragedy*, or The Pleasures and Perils of Rhetoric', in *Elizabethan Theatre*, Stratford-upon-Avon Studies 9, ed. J. R. Brown and B. A. Harris (London, 1966), pp. 59–86

Bate, Jonathan, 'The Performance of Revenge: *Titus Andronicus* and *The Spanish Tragedy*', in *The Show Within: Dramatic and other Insets*, ed. François Laroque (Montpellier, 1990), 267–83

Bercovitch, Sacvan, 'Love and Strife in Kyd's *Spanish Tragedy*', *SEL*, 9 (1969), 215–29

Bowers, Fredson T., *Elizabethan Revenge Tragedy* (Princeton, 1940), chs. 1–3

Braden, Gordon, *Renaissance Tragedy and the Senecan Tradition* (New Haven, 1985)

Broude, Ronald, 'Time, Truth, and Right in *The Spanish Tragedy*', *SP*, 68 (1971), 130–45

Clemen, Wolfgang, *English Tragedy before Shakespeare* (London, 1961), pp. 100–12, 267–77

Daalder, Joost, 'The Role of "Senex" in Kyd's *The Spanish Tragedy'*, *Comparative Drama*, 20 (1986), 247–60

Dollimore, Jonathan, *Radical Tragedy: Religion, Ideology and Power in the Drama of Shakespeare and His Contemporaries* (Brighton, 1984)

Edwards, Philip, *Thomas Kyd and Early Elizabethan Tragedy* (London, 1966)

'Thrusting Elysium into Hell: the Originality of *The Spanish Tragedy'*, in *The Elizabethan Theatre*, XI, ed. A. L. Magnusson and C. E. McGee (Ontario, Canada, 1990), 117–32

Eliot, T. S., 'Seneca in Elizabethan Translation', *Selected Essays* (London, 1932), pp. 65–108

Freeman, Arthur, *Thomas Kyd: facts and problems* (Oxford, 1967)

Hallett, Charles A., and Elaine S. Hallett, *The Revenger's Madness: A Study of Revenge Tragedy Motifs* (Lincoln, Nebraska, 1980)

Hamilton, Donna B., '*The Spanish Tragedy*: a speaking picture', *ELR*, 4 (1974), 203–17

Hattaway, Michael, *Elizabethan Popular Theatre: plays in performance* (London, 1982)

Hill, Eugene D., 'Senecan and Vergilian Perspectives in *The Spanish Tragedy'*, *ELR*, 15 (1985), 143–65. Reprinted in *Renaissance Historicism: Selections from 'English Literary Renaissance'*, ed. A. F. Kinney and D. S. Collins (Amherst, Mass., 1987)

Howard, Tony, 'Renaissance Drama Productions', *RORD*, 21 (1978), 64–5 and *RORD*, 26 (1983), 76–7

Hunter, G. K., 'Ironies of Justice in *The Spanish Tragedy'*, *Renaissance Drama*, 8 (1965), 89–104

Jensen, Ejner J., 'Kyd's *Spanish Tragedy*: the play explains itself', *JEGP*, 64 (1965), 7–16

Johnson, S. F., '*The Spanish Tragedy* or Babylon Revisited', in *Essays on Shakespeare and Elizabethan Drama in Honour of Hardin Craig*, ed. Richard Hosley (London, 1963), pp. 23–36

Jongh, Nicholas de, '*The Spanish Tragedy* at the Cottesloe', *Plays and Players*, Issue No. 351 (December, 1982), 24–5

Knutson, Roslyn A., 'The Influence of the Repertory System on the Revival and Revision of *The Spanish Tragedy* and *Dr. Faustus'*, *ELR* 18 (1988), 257–74

McAlindon, T. E., *English Renaissance Tragedy* (London, 1986), esp. ch. 2

'*Tamburlaine the Great* and *The Spanish Tragedy*: the Genesis of a Tradition', *Huntington Library Quarterly*, 45 (1982), 59–81

McMillin, Scott, 'The Figure of Silence in *The Spanish Tragedy'*, *ELH* 39 (1972), 27–48

Mulryne, J. R., 'Nationality and Language in Thomas Kyd's '*The Spanish Tragedy*', in *Travel and Drama in Shakespeare's Time*, ed. Jean-Pierre Maquerlot and Michele Willems (Cambridge, 1996), pp. 87–105

Murray, Peter B., *Thomas Kyd* (New York, 1969)

Neill, Michael, *Issues of Death: Mortality and Identity in English Renaissance Tragedy* (Oxford, 1997)

Rowan, D. F., 'The Staging of *The Spanish Tragedy*', in *The Elizabethan Theatre V*, ed. G. R. Hibbard (London, 1975), 112–23

Shapiro, James, ' "Tragedy Naturally Performed": Kyd's Representation of Violence', in *Staging the Renaissance: Reinterpretations of Elizabethan and Jacobean Drama*, ed. David Scott Kastan and Peter Stallybrass (London, 1991), 99–113

Siemon, James R., 'Dialogual Formalism: Word, Object and Action in *The Spanish Tragedy*', *Medieval and Renaissance Drama*, IV (1990), 87–115

Siemon, James R., 'Sporting Kyd', *ELR* 24 (1994), 553–82.

Smith, Molly, 'The Theater and the Scaffold: Death as Spectacle in *The Spanish Tragedy*', *SEL*, 32 (1992), 217–32

Stilling, Roger, *Love and Death in Renaissance Tragedy* (Baton Rouge, Louisiana, 1976)

Tomlinson, T. B., *A Study of Elizabethan and Jacobean Tragedy* (Melbourne and Cambridge, 1964), ch. 4

Watson, Robert N., 'Tragedy' in *The Cambridge Companion to English Renaissance Drama*, ed. A. R. Braunmuller and Michael Hattaway (Cambridge, 1990)

White, Martin, *Renaissance Drama in Action* (London: Routledge, 1998)

THE

SPANISH TRAGE-
die, Containing the lamentable
end of *Don Horatio*, and *Bel-imperia*:
with the pittifull death of
olde *Hieronimo*.

Newly corrected and amended of such grosse faults as
passed in the first impression.

AT LONDON
Printed by *Edward Allde*, for
Edward White.*

[DRAMATIS PERSONAE

GHOST OF ANDREA
REVENGE
KING OF SPAIN
CYPRIAN, DUKE OF CASTILE, *his brother*
LORENZO, *the Duke's son*
BEL-IMPERIA, *Lorenzo's sister*
GENERAL *of the Spanish Army*

VICEROY OF PORTUGAL
PEDRO, *his brother*
BALTHAZAR, *his son*
ALEXANDRO ⎱ *Portuguese noblemen*
VILLUPPO ⎰
AMBASSADOR *of Portugal*

HIERONIMO, *Knight Marshal of Spain*
ISABELLA, *his wife*
HORATIO, *their son*

PEDRINGANO, *servant to Bel-imperia*
SERBERINE, *servant to Balthazar*
CHRISTOPHIL, *servant to Lorenzo*
BAZULTO, *an old man*

Page *to Lorenzo*, Three Watchmen, Messenger, Deputy, Hangman, Maid to *Isabella*, Two Portuguese, Servant, Three Citizens, Portuguese Nobles, Soldiers, Officers, Attendants, Halberdiers

Three Knights, Three Kings, a Drummer *in the first Dumb-show*, Hymen, Two Torch-bearers *in the second Dumb-show*

In the 'Additions':
PEDRO ⎱ *Hieronimo's servants*
JAQUES ⎰
BAZARDO, *a Painter*]

3

THE SPANISH TRAGEDY

Act I, Scene i

Enter the Ghost of ANDREA, *and with him* REVENGE

ANDREA
　　When this eternal substance of my soul
　　Did live imprisoned in my wanton flesh,
　　Each in their function serving other's need,
　　I was a courtier in the Spanish court.
　　My name was Don Andrea, my descent,　　　　　　　5
　　Though not ignoble, yet inferior far
　　To gracious fortunes of my tender youth:
　　For there in prime and pride of all my years,
　　By duteous service and deserving love,
　　In secret I possessed a worthy dame,　　　　　　　10
　　Which hight sweet Bel-imperia by name.
　　But in the harvest of my summer joys
　　Death's winter nipped the blossoms of my bliss,
　　Forcing divorce betwixt my love and me.
　　For in the late conflict with Portingale　　　　　　15

---

1 s.d. Hattaway (p. 115) notes that this entry may have been from the stage trap, as lines in Dekker's *The Seven Deadly Sins of London* referring to 'the Ghost in Jeronimo' imply.

1 ff. These opening lines were often parodied in later Elizabethan plays. Edwards quotes Beaumont's *The Knight of the Burning Pestle* (first performed 1607), V. i: 'When I was mortal, this my costive corpse/Did lap up figs and raisins in the Strand.' Hill (pp. 147–8) interprets the tone of ll. 1–10 as that of 'no virtuously mourning ghost, but a slick Spanish Don, boasting of his amorous prowess'.

8 *prime* spring-time

8 *pride* the most flourishing condition (*O.E.D.*)

10 *possessed* made love to

10–11 *In secret . . . by name* The details of this intrigue are never made plain, perhaps to avoid an unfavourable estimate of Bel-imperia. It is, however, mentioned again at II, i, 45–8, III, x, 54–5 and III, xiv, 111–12. Its clandestine nature anticipates the Horatio/Bel-imperia relationship, making for one more parallel between Andrea and Horatio. It also predicts the uneasy tensions between opposites of the play to come (see McAlindon, p. 58).

11 *hight* was called

13 *nipped* destroyed by frost

14 *divorce* separation

15 *Portingale* Portugal

My valour drew me into danger's mouth,
Till life to death made passage through my wounds.
When I was slain, my soul descended straight
To pass the flowing stream of Acheron:
But churlish Charon, only boatman there,   20
Said that my rites of burial not performed,
I might not sit amongst his passengers.
Ere Sol had slept three nights in Thetis' lap
And slaked his smoking chariot in her flood,
By Don Horatio, our Knight Marshal's son,   25
My funerals and obsequies were done.
Then was the ferryman of hell content
To pass me over to the slimy strond,
That leads to fell Avernus' ugly waves:
There, pleasing Cerberus with honeyed speech,   30
I passed the perils of the foremost porch.
Not far from hence, amidst ten thousand souls,
Sat Minos, Aeacus, and Rhadamanth,
To whom no sooner 'gan I make approach,
To crave a passport for my wandering ghost,   35

18 ff. This description of the underworld derives from *Aeneid* book VI, though
    Kyd has altered the details of Virgil's description. For a full discussion see Boas,
    pp. 394–5.
19 *Acheron* a river of the lower world, identified here with Styx where Charon was
    ferryman
23 *Sol* the sun
23 *Thetis* daughter of Nereus, a Homeric sea-god; here, the sea
24 *slaked* extinguished the flame of
24 *her flood* the sea
25 *Knight Marshal* a legal official of the English royal household 'who had judicial
    cognizance of transgressions "within the king's house and verge", i.e. within a
    radius of twelve miles from the king's palace' (*O.E.D.*, Marshal sb. 6b).
    Hieronimo's judicial responsibilities are insisted upon even before Horatio's
    murder.
28 *strond* shore
29 *fell* cruel, deadly
29 *Avernus* the lake near Puteoli thought to serve as entrance to the underworld
30 *Cerberus* the monstrous three-headed dog, guardian of the underworld
31 *porch* place of entry
33 *Minos, Aeacus, Rhadamanth* judges of the underworld
35 *passport* safe-conduct, letters of protection

But Minos, in graven leaves of lottery,
Drew forth the manner of my life and death.
'This knight', quoth he, 'both lived and died in love,
And for his love tried fortune of the wars,
And by war's fortune lost both love and life.'   40
'Why then,' said Aeacus, 'convey him hence,
To walk with lovers in our fields of love,
And spend the course of everlasting time
Under green myrtle trees and cypress shades.'
'No, no,' said Rhadamanth, 'it were not well   45
With loving souls to place a martialist:
He died in war, and must to martial fields,
Where wounded Hector lives in lasting pain,
And Achilles' Myrmidons do scour the plain.'
Then Minos, mildest censor of the three,   50
Made this device to end the difference:
'Send him,' quoth he, 'to our infernal king,
To doom him as best seems his majesty.'
To this effect my passport straight was drawn.
In keeping on my way to Pluto's court,   55
Through dreadful shades of ever-glooming night,
I saw more sights than thousand tongues can tell,
Or pens can write, or mortal hearts can think.
Three ways there were: that on the right-hand side
Was ready way unto the foresaid fields   60
Where lovers live and bloody martialists,
But either sort contained within his bounds.

36 *graven leaves of lottery* not clear. Lots are drawn in Virgil to settle where the
   dead will spend the after-life, but here it seems that Minos is, additionally,
   reading from some account of Andrea's past. Edwards comments: '*Drew forth* (l.
   37) is best interpreted literally and we must suppose that Minos draws from his
   urn the lottery slip on which was engraved the manner of life which Andrea has
   by now fulfilled, i.e. what has been his lot'.
36-47 Hill (p. 149) detects in these lines, especially ll. 38 and 45, 'the prissy
   pedantry of these judges'.
46 *martialist* warrior
49 *Achilles' Myrmidons* followers of the warrior Achilles in Homer; killers of
   Hector (l. 48)
49 *scour* range speedily over
50 *censor* judge
52 *infernal* underworld
53 *doom* give judgment on
55 *Pluto* king of the underworld
56 *ever-glooming* always dark and threatening
62 *his* its own

The left-hand path, declining fearfully,
Was ready downfall to the deepest hell,
Where bloody Furies shakes their whips of steel,   65
And poor Ixion turns an endless wheel;
Where usurers are choked with melting gold,
And wantons are embraced with ugly snakes,
And murderers groan with never-killing wounds,
And perjured wights scalded in boiling lead,   70
And all foul sins with torments overwhelmed.
'Twixt these two ways I trod the middle path,
Which brought me to the fair Elysian green,
In midst whereof there stands a stately tower,
The walls of brass, the gates of adamant.   75
Here finding Pluto with his Proserpine,
I showed my passport, humbled on my knee;
Whereat fair Proserpine began to smile,
And begged that only she might give my doom.
Pluto was pleased, and sealed it with a kiss.   80
Forthwith, Revenge, she rounded thee in th'ear,

63–71 Lorenzo and his confederates are doomed to this region of hell at the play's
        end, while Horatio, Bel-imperia, Isabella and Hieronimo take the alternative
        path (for lovers and martialists). See IV, v, 17 ff.
63 *declining* sloping down
64 *downfall* precipice, gulf
65 *Furies* mythical avengers of crime
66 *Ixion* punished on a treadmill for seeking Hera's love
70 *wights* persons
72 Virgil specifies two paths only (*Aeneid VI*, 540–43); Kyd's mention of a 'middle
        path' may be linked with his creation of a placeless Andrea.
73 *Elysian green* Elysium is the abode of the blessed in the after-life; Virgil places
        it in the underworld.
75 *adamant* very hard stone; diamond
76 McAlindon (p. 57) notes that the union of Pluto and Proserpine was 'one of the
        most famous agreements in classical mythology', effecting a reconciliation of
        Pluto and Ceres, and therefore of the ultimate opposites of life and death,
        summer and winter. Hill (pp. 149–50) reminds us that Proserpine was the
        figure to whom Aeneas presented the Golden Bough in the *Aeneid*; Andrea's
        presentation of his passport makes him an alternative Aeneas, but one deprived
        of understanding or purpose.
76 *Proserpine* the Greek Persephone, consort of Dis (or Pluto), queen of the
        underworld
77 *humbled on my knee* kneeling in humility
79 *doom* sentence
81 *rounded* whispered

And bade thee lead me through the gates of horn,
Where dreams have passage in the silent night.
No sooner had she spoke but we were here,
I wot not how, in twinkling of an eye.   85
REVENGE
Then know, Andrea, that thou art arrived
Where thou shalt see the author of thy death,
Don Balthazar, the prince of Portingale,
Deprived of life by Bel-imperia.
Here sit we down to see the mystery,   90
And serve for Chorus in this tragedy.

Act I, Scene ii

Enter SPANISH KING, GENERAL, CASTILE, HIERONIMO

KING
Now say, Lord General, how fares our camp?
GENERAL
All well, my sovereign liege, except some few
That are deceased by fortune of the war.
KING
But what portends thy cheerful countenance,
And posting to our presence thus in haste?   5
Speak man, hath fortune given us victory?
GENERAL
Victory, my liege, and that with little loss.
KING
Our Portingals will pay us tribute then?

82 *horn* ed. (Hor: *1592*)
82 *gates of horn* The gate of horn in *Aeneid* VI (modelled on Homer) is the gate
   through which *true* dreams or visions pass, as against the ivory gate of *false*
   dreams. Hill (p. 150) notes that Aeneas passed through the gates of ivory in
   making his exit from the underworld.
85 *wot* know
86-9 The audience's knowledge that these events will take place has an important
   bearing on their attitude to the action and the characters in the main play.
90 *mystery* events yet to be revealed, of a special significance
1 *camp* army in the field
1-21 The opening lines of this scene have a calculated air of light optimism and
   even complacency: ironic in view of our knowledge that catastrophe is to follow.
5 *posting* speeding
8 *Portingals* Portuguese
8 *tribute* tribute-money

GENERAL

   Tribute and wonted homage therewithal.

KING

   Then blest be heaven, and guider of the heavens,   10
   From whose fair influence such justice flows.

CASTILE

   O multum dilecte Deo, tibi militat aether,
   Et conjuratae curvato poplite gentes
   Succumbunt: recti soror est victoria juris.

KING

   Thanks to my loving brother of Castile.   15
   But General, unfold in brief discourse
   Your form of battle and your war's success,
   That adding all the pleasure of thy news
   Unto the height of former happiness,
   With deeper wage and greater dignity   20
   We may reward thy blissful chivalry.

GENERAL

   Where Spain and Portingale do jointly knit
   Their frontiers, leaning on each other's bound,
   There met our armies in their proud array:
   Both furnished well, both full of hope and fear,   25
   Both menacing alike with daring shows,
   Both vaunting sundry colours of device,
   Both cheerly sounding trumpets, drums and fifes,
   Both raising dreadful clamours to the sky,
   That valleys, hills, and rivers made rebound,   30
   And heaven itself was frighted with the sound.

12–14 'O one much loved of God, for thee the heavens contend, and the united
    peoples fall down on bended knee: victory is sister to just right.' Boas indicates
    the lines are adapted from Claudian's *De Tertio Consulatu Honorii*, 96–8.

13 *poplite* ed. (*poplito 1592*)

16 *unfold* explain

20 *deeper wage* richer reward

21 *chivalry* skill in arms

22–84 The General's account of the battle (in accordance with Kyd's narrative
    patterning) expands that of Andrea at I, i, 15 ff., and anticipates both the
    distorted version by Villuppo (I, iii, 59 ff.) and Horatio's corrective account at
    I, iv, 9 ff. It serves both as 'good theatre' in the elaborate theatrical vein enjoyed
    by Elizabethans, and also to establish an unbiased perspective on events from
    which the rest of the plot springs.

23 *bound* boundary

25 *furnished* equipped

27 *vaunting* displaying proudly

27 *colours of device* heraldic banners

Our battles both were pitched in squadron form,
Each corner strongly fenced with wings of shot;
But ere we joined and came to push of pike,
I brought a squadron of our readiest shot   35
From out our rearward to begin the fight:
They brought another wing to encounter us.
Meanwhile, our ordnance played on either side,
And captains strove to have their valours tried.
Don Pedro, their chief horsemen's colonel,   40
Did with his cornet bravely make attempt
To break the order of our battle ranks:
But Don Rogero, worthy man of war,
Marched forth against him with our musketeers,
And stopped the malice of his fell approach.   45
While they maintain hot skirmish to and fro,
Both battles join and fall to handy blows,
Their violent shot resembling th'ocean's rage,
When, roaring loud, and with a swelling tide,
It beats upon the rampiers of huge rocks,   50
And gapes to swallow neighbour-bounding lands.
Now while Bellona rageth here and there,
Thick storms of bullets rain like winter's hail,
And shivered lances dark the troubled air.
                Pede pes et cuspide cuspis;   55

32 *battles* forces
32 *squadron form* in a square formation
33 *fenced* defended, reinforced
33 *wings of shot* soldiers carrying firearms placed on the outer edges of the
   formation
34 *push of pike* hand-to-hand fighting
38 *ordnance* ed. (ordinance *1592*) heavy artillery
38 *played* directed their fire
40 *colonel* ed. (Corlonell *1592*) three syllables
41 *cornet* a squadron of cavalry
45 *malice* danger, harm
47 *handy* hand-to-hand
48 *shot* shooting, exchange of fire (presumably at close quarters)
50 *rampiers* ramparts
51 *neighbour-bounding* neighbouring, on its margin
52 *Bellona* Roman goddess of war
53 *rain* ed. (ran *1592*)
54 *dark* darken
55–6 'Foot against foot and spear against spear, arms ring on arms and man is
   assailed by man.' Boas says the Latin is taken partly from Statius (*Thebais*, viii,
   399) and, quoting Schick, partly structured on analogies in Virgil and Curtius.

Arma sonant armis, vir petiturque viro.
On every side drop captains to the ground,
And soldiers, some ill-maimed, some slain outright:
Here falls a body scindered from his head,
There legs and arms lie bleeding on the grass,   60
Mingled with weapons and unbowelled steeds,
That scattering overspread the purple plain.
In all this turmoil, three long hours and more,
The victory to neither part inclined,
Till Don Andrea with his brave lanciers   65
In their main battle made so great a breach
That, half dismayed, the multitude retired:
But Balthazar, the Portingales' young prince,
Brought rescue, and encouraged them to stay.
Here-hence the fight was eagerly renewed,   70
And in that conflict was Andrea slain –
Brave man at arms, but weak to Balthazar.
Yet while the prince, insulting over him,
Breathed out proud vaunts, sounding to our reproach,
Friendship and hardy valour joined in one   75
Pricked forth Horatio, our Knight Marshal's son,
To challenge forth that prince in single fight.
Not long between these twain the fight endured,
But straight the prince was beaten from his horse,
And forced to yield him prisoner to his foe: 80
When he was taken, all the rest they fled,
And our carbines pursued them to the death,
Till, Phoebus waning to the western deep,

56 *Arma* ed. (*Anni* 1592)
56 *armis* ed. (*annis* 1592)
58 *ill-maimed* badly injured
59 *scindered* sundered
62 *purple* blood-red, covered in blood
65 *lanciers* (two syllables) lancers
70 *Here-hence* as a result of this (*O.E.D.*, 1)
72 *man at arms* specifically, a mounted soldier
72 A reminiscence, in keeping with the heroic manner of these lines, of references
   to defeated warriors in Homer.
73 *insulting* exulting
74 *sounding to* tending to, inferring (*O.E.D.*, 5a)
76 *Pricked forth* spurred on
80 *him* himself
82 *carbines* presumably soldiers carrying these weapons (*O.E.D.* has no example)
83 *Phoebus* the sun
83 *waning* ed. (*wauing* 1592)
83 *deep* the sea

Our trumpeters were charged to sound retreat.

KING

Thanks good Lord General for these good news;   85
And for some argument of more to come,
Take this and wear it for thy sovereign's sake.
                                        Give him his chain
But tell me now, hast thou confirmed a peace?

GENERAL

No peace, my liege, but peace conditional,
That if with homage tribute be well paid,   90
The fury of your forces will be stayed:
And to this peace their viceroy hath subscribed,
                                        Give the KING *a paper*
And made a solemn vow that, during life,
His tribute shall be truly paid to Spain.

KING

These words, these deeds, become thy person well.   95
But now, Knight Marshal, frolic with thy king,
For 'tis thy son that wins this battle's prize.

HIERONIMO

Long may he live to serve my sovereign liege,
And soon decay unless he serve my liege.
                                        A tucket afar off

KING

Nor thou, nor he, shall die without reward.   100
What means the warning of this trumpet's sound?

GENERAL

This tells me that your grace's men of war,
Such as war's fortune hath reserved from death,
Come marching on towards your royal seat,
To show themselves before your majesty,   105
For so I gave in charge at my depart.
Whereby by demonstration shall appear,
That all (except three hundred or few more)

---

86 *argument* token
89 *but* except
91 *stayed* restrained, halted
92 *subscribed* signed his name
96 *frolic* rejoice, be happy
99 *decay* fail in health and fortune
101 *the* ed. (this *1592*)
108 This calm writing-off of 300 men perhaps underlines what we know to be the false complacency of the Spanish court. Compare the opening speeches of *Much Ado*.

Are safe returned and by their foes enriched.

The Army enters; BALTHAZAR, *between* LORENZO *and* HORATIO,
captive

KING
    A gladsome sight! I long to see them here.   110
                                 They enter and pass by
    Was that the warlike prince of Portingale,
    That by our nephew was in triumph led?

GENERAL
    It was, my liege, the prince of Portingale.

KING
    But what was he that on the other side
    Held him by th'arm as partner of the prize?   115

HIERONIMO
    That was my son, my gracious sovereign,
    Of whom, though from his tender infancy
    My loving thoughts did never hope but well,
    He never pleased his father's eyes till now,
    Nor filled my heart with overcloying joys.   120

KING
    Go let them march once more about these walls,
    That staying them we may confer and talk
    With our brave prisoner and his double guard.
    Hieronimo, it greatly pleaseth us,
    That in our victory thou have a share,   125
    By virtue of thy worthy son's exploit.
                            Enter [*the Army*] *again*
    Bring hither the young prince of Portingale:
    The rest march on, but ere they be dismissed,
    We will bestow on every soldier
    Two ducats, and on every leader ten,   130

109 s.d. The double entry of the army (here and after l. 126) complements the high
      verbal flourish of the General's speech and extends the air of martial grandeur
      and confidence; it also permits the theatrical display so dear to Elizabethans.
110 s.d. This action probably resembles the 'passage over the stage', used in a
      number of Elizabethan plays, by which players entered the yard of the theatre,
      marched across the stage and exited at the opposite side of the yard.
111ff. Kyd's very strong sense of dramatic structure brings the three principal
      antagonists together at their first entry; the later enmity between Lorenzo and
      Horatio is visually suggested by each laying claim to the prisoner Balthazar.
120 *overcloying* causing surfeit, satiating
122 *staying* stopping
129–31 (lineation ed. We . . . ducats/And . . . know/Our . . . them *1592*)

That they may know our largess welcomes them.
Exeunt all [the Army] but
BALTHAZAR, LORENZO, HORATIO

Welcome, Don Balthazar, welcome, nephew,
And thou, Horatio, thou art welcome too.
Young prince, although thy father's hard misdeeds,
In keeping back the tribute that he owes,   135
Deserve but evil measure at our hands,
Yet shalt thou know that Spain is honourable.

BALTHAZAR
The trespass that my father made in peace
Is now controlled by fortune of the wars;
And cards once dealt, it boots not ask why so.   140
His men are slain, a weakening to his realm,
His colours seized, a blot unto his name,
His son distressed, a corsive to his heart:
Those punishments may clear his late offence.

KING
Ay, Balthazar, if he observe this truce,   145
Our peace will grow the stronger for these wars.
Meanwhile live thou, though not in liberty,
Yet free from bearing any servile yoke;
For in our hearing thy deserts were great,
And in our sight thyself art gracious.   150

BALTHAZAR
And I shall study to deserve this grace.

KING
But tell me, for their holding makes me doubt,
To which of these twain art thou prisoner?

LORENZO
To me, my liege.

HORATIO   To me, my sovereign.

131 *largess* money and gifts bestowed by a king
139 *controlled* brought to an end
140 *boots* profits   142 *colours* standards, flags
143 *distressed* taken prisoner
143 *corsive* corrosive (a destructive substance)
144 *clear* erase
144 *late* previous, past
152 *their holding* the way they hold you
152 ff. Clemen (p. 101) points out that the scene from this point corresponds to the
    familiar Elizabethan 'tribunal scene' in which a dispute between two nobles is
    arbitrated by the king. (Compare *e.g. Richard II*, I, i.) Kyd's handling of this
    conventional situation is much more flexible dramatically than that of his
    predecessors.

LORENZO

   This hand first took his courser by the reins.   155

HORATIO

   But first my lance did put him from his horse.

LORENZO

   I seized his weapon, and enjoyed it first.

HORATIO

   But first I forced him lay his weapons down.

KING

   Let go his arm, upon our privilege.   *[They] let him go*

   Say, worthy prince, to whether didst thou yield?   160

BALTHAZAR

   To him in courtesy, to this perforce:

   He spake me fair, this other gave me strokes;

   He promised life, this other threatened death;

   He wan my love, this other conquered me:

   And truth to say I yield myself to both.   165

HIERONIMO

   But that I know your grace for just and wise,

   And might seem partial in this difference,

   Enforced by nature and by law of arms

   My tongue should plead for young Horatio's right.

   He hunted well that was a lion's death,   170

   Not he that in a garment wore his skin:

   So hares may pull dead lions by the beard.

KING

   Content thee, Marshal, thou shalt have no wrong;

   And for thy sake thy son shall want no right.

   Will both abide the censure of my doom?   175

LORENZO

   I crave no better than your grace awards.

HORATIO

   Nor I, although I sit beside my right.

KING

   Then by my judgment thus your strife shall end:

159 *privilege* the king's prerogative
160 *whether* which of the two
164 *wan* won
167 *partial* guilty of favouritism
170–2 Hieronimo argues that Horatio deserves credit as the true conqueror of
    Balthazar. The reference in l. 171 derives, as Edwards shows, from the Fourth
    Fable of Avian concerning as ass who disports himself in a lion's skin he has
    found. Line 172 is proverbial; even timid hares may beard a *dead* lion.
175 *censure of my doom* the outcome of my judgment
177 *sit beside* forgo (Edwards)

You both deserve and both shall have reward.
Nephew, thou took'st his weapon and his horse,   180
His weapons and his horse are thy reward.
Horatio, thou didst force him first to yield,
His ransom therefore is thy valour's fee:
Appoint the sum as you shall both agree.
But nephew, thou shalt have the prince in guard,   185
For thine estate best fitteth such a guest:
Horatio's house were small for all his train.
Yet in regard thy substance passeth his,
And that just guerdon may befall desert,
To him we yield the armour of the prince.   190
How likes Don Balthazar of this device?

BALTHAZAR

Right well my liege, if this proviso were,
That Don Horatio bear us company,
Whom I admire and love for chivalry.

KING

Horatio, leave him not that loves thee so.   195
Now let us hence to see our soldiers paid,
And feast our prisoner as our friendly guest.   *Exeunt*

Act I, Scene iii

Enter VICEROY, ALEXANDRO, VILLUPPO [, *Attendants*]

VICEROY

Is our ambassador despatched for Spain?

ALEXANDRO

Two days, my liege, are passed since his depart.

VICEROY

And tribute payment gone along with him?

ALEXANDRO

Ay my good lord.

---

187 Horatio's social standing (like Hieronimo's) is emphatically lower than that of
     Lorenzo and Bel-imperia (and of course Balthazar). See also II, iv, 61 and III,
     x, 57.
188 *in regard* since
189 *that* in order that
189 *guerdon* reward
190 *him* Horatio

VICEROY

Then rest we here awhile in our unrest,   5
And feed our sorrows with some inward sighs,
For deepest cares break never into tears.
But wherefore sit I in a regal throne?
This better fits a wretch's endless moan.

Falls to the ground

Yet this is higher than my fortunes reach,   10
And therefore better than my state deserves.
Ay, ay, this earth, image of melancholy,
Seeks him whom fates adjudge to misery:
Here let me lie, now am I at the lowest.

    Qui jacet in terra, non habet unde cadat.   15
    In me consumpsit vires fortuna nocendo,
    Nil superest ut jam possit obesse magis.

Yes, Fortune may bereave me of my crown:
Here, take it now; let Fortune do her worst,
She will not rob me of this sable weed: 20
O no, she envies none but pleasant things.
Such is the folly of despiteful chance!

5 ff. The Viceroy's speech contrasts with the self-congratulation of the Spanish
    King, and anticipates Hieronimo's similar grief over the loss of a son. Clemen
    (p. 269) draws attention to Kyd's dramatically alert transformation in these
    lines of the standard 'lament speech'. Compare the King's lines in *Richard II*,
    III, ii, 144 ff. It may be, as Hill (p. 154, fn. 25) suggests, that the Viceroy's
    weakness of spirit correlates with English low esteem of the Portuguese after
    their failure to rise in support of Drake's mission to Lisbon in 1589.
9 s.d. follows l. 11 in *1592*
10 'My circumstances are even worse than this suggests.'
11 *state* condition, situation
12 *image of melancholy* Melancholy is the bodily 'humour' (responsible for a
    person's temperament) that corresponds to the element earth, one of the four
    elements (the others are air, fire and water) that make up all created things.
15–17 'If one lies on the ground, one has no further to fall. Towards me Fortune
    has exhausted her power to injure; there is nothing further that can happen to
    me.' The first line is borrowed from Alanus de Insulis, *Lib. Parab.*, cap. 2, l. 19,
    the second from Seneca's *Agamemnon* l. 698, while the third is probably Kyd's
    own composition. (See W. P. Mustard, *PQ*, 5 (1926), 85–6.)
20 *sable weed* black costume
21 *envies* feels ill-will towards
22 *despiteful* malicious

Fortune is blind and sees not my deserts,
So is she deaf and hears not my laments:
And could she hear, yet is she wilful mad,   25
And therefore will not pity my distress.
Suppose that she could pity me, what then?
What help can be expected at her hands,
Whose foot is standing on a rolling stone,
And mind more mutable than fickle winds?   30
Why wail I then, where's hope of no redress?
O yes, complaining makes my grief seem less.
My late ambition hath distained my faith,
My breach of faith occasioned bloody wars,
Those bloody wars have spent my treasure,   35
And with my treasure my people's blood,
And with their blood, my joy and best beloved,
My best beloved, my sweet and only son.
O wherefore went I not to war myself?
The cause was mine, I might have died for both: 40
My years were mellow, his but young and green,
My death were natural, but his was forced.

ALEXANDRO
No doubt, my liege, but still the prince survives.
VICEROY
Survives! ay, where?
ALEXANDRO
In Spain, a prisoner by mischance of war.   45
VICEROY
Then they have slain him for his father's fault.
ALEXANDRO
That were a breach to common law of arms.

23–30 In the emblem books, Fortune is normally depicted as blind, sometimes as
    deaf, and frequently as standing on a rolling sphere; all to express her lack of
    discrimination and changeableness. The Viceroy's complaint of Fortune
    contributes to the play's preoccupation with justice and retribution. Lines
    33–42 are the Viceroy's attempt to construct a rational (and therefore 'just')
    explanation for what has happened, and so to rationalise Fortune.
25 *wilful mad* deliberately closed to reason
29 *is* ed. (not in *1592*)
30 *mutable* ever-changing
33 *distained* sullied
35, 36 *treasure* Edwards says tri-syllabic: 'treas-u-er'
42 *forced* against the course of nature
46 *fault* crime, wrongdoing

VICEROY
    They reck no laws that meditate revenge.
ALEXANDRO
    His ransom's worth will stay from foul revenge.
VICEROY
    No, if he lived the news would soon be here.   50
ALEXANDRO
    Nay, evil news fly faster still than good.
VICEROY
    Tell me no more of news, for he is dead.
VILLUPPO
    My sovereign, pardon the author of ill news,
    And I'll bewray the fortune of thy son.
VICEROY
    Speak on, I'll guerdon thee whate'er it be: 55
    Mine ear is ready to receive ill news,
    My heart grown hard 'gainst mischief's battery;
    Stand up I say, and tell thy tale at large.
VILLUPPO
    Then hear that truth which these mine eyes have seen.
    When both the armies were in battle joined,   60
    Don Balthazar, amidst the thickest troops,
    To win renown did wondrous feats of arms:
    Amongst the rest I saw him hand to hand
    In single fight with their Lord General;
    Till Alexandro, that here counterfeits   65
    Under the colour of a duteous friend,
    Discharged his pistol at the prince's back,
    As though he would have slain their general.
    But therewithal Don Balthazar fell down,
    And when he fell, then we began to fly: 70
    But had he lived, the day had sure been ours.

48 *reck* heed
48 That revenge was by nature lawless was the accepted Elizabethan attitude (see
    Bowers, esp. pp. 3–14).
49 *stay* restrain
53 *author* one who transmits; or one who lends his authority to, vouches for
54 *bewray* reveal
55 *guerdon* reward
57 *mischief* misfortune
65–71 Broude (p. 134) explains the pertinence of the Portuguese scenes in terms
    of the Renaissance *topos* of the calumniated courtier, citing the *Calumny* of
    Lucian of Samosata as a possible source.
66 *colour* pretence

ALEXANDRO

O wicked forgery! O traitorous miscreant!

VICEROY

Hold thou thy peace! But now, Villuppo, say,
Where then became the carcase of my son?

VILLUPPO

I saw them drag it to the Spanish tents.   75

VICEROY

Ay, ay, my nightly dreams have told me this.
Thou false, unkind, unthankful, traitorous beast,
Wherein had Balthazar offended thee,
That thou shouldst thus betray him to our foes?
Was't Spanish gold that bleared so thine eyes   80
That thou couldst see no part of our deserts?
Perchance because thou art Terceira's lord,
Thou hadst some hope to wear this diadem,
If first my son and then myself were slain:
But thy ambitious thought shall break thy neck.   85
Ay, this was it that made thee spill his blood,
          Take the crown and put it on again
But I'll now wear it till thy blood be spilt.

ALEXANDRO

Vouchsafe, dread sovereign, to hear me speak.

VICEROY

Away with him, his sight is second hell;
Keep him till we determine of his death.   90
          [*Exeunt Attendants with* ALEXANDRO]
If Balthazar be dead, he shall not live.
Villuppo, follow us for thy reward.   *Exit* VICEROY

VILLUPPO

Thus have I with an envious, forged tale
Deceived the king, betrayed mine enemy,
And hope for guerdon of my villainy.   *Exit*   95

---

72 *forgery* falsehood, fabrication
72 *miscreant* villain, rascal
82 *Terceira's lord* Boas says that Alexandro was apparently *Capitão Donatario* of
    Terceira, an island in the Azores group, and would because of this position
    enjoy virtually despotic powers. The title was given to the first discoverers and
    colonisers of overseas territories and was hereditary.
83 *diadem* ed. (Diadome *1592*)
93 *envious* malicious
93-5 The villain's explicit confession seems awkward to modern readers; it
    remained a convention widely acceptable in the Elizabethan theatre. Compare
    e.g. Flamineo in *The White Devil*, IV, ii, 242-6.

Act I, Scene iv

Enter HORATIO *and* BEL-IMPERIA

BEL-IMPERIA
Signior Horatio, this is the place and hour
Wherein I must entreat thee to relate
The circumstance of Don Andrea's death,
Who, living, was my garland's sweetest flower,
And in his death hath buried my delights.   5
HORATIO
For love of him and service to yourself,
I nill refuse this heavy doleful charge.
Yet tears and sighs, I fear will hinder me.
When both our armies were enjoined in fight,
Your worthy chevalier amidst the thick'st,   10
For glorious cause still aiming at the fairest,
Was at the last by young Don Balthazar
Encountered hand to hand: their fight was long,
Their hearts were great, their clamours menacing,
Their strength alike, their strokes both dangerous.   15
But wrathful Nemesis, that wicked power,
Envying at Andrea's praise and worth,
Cut short his life, to end his praise and worth.
She, she herself, disguised in armour's mask,
(As Pallas was before proud Pergamus)   20

6–43 Horatio's account of the battle gives the personal angle, as against the
    General's more objective description. Contrast the emotionalism of many lines
    in this speech with the General's technicalities (esp. I, ii, 32 ff.).
 7 *nill* will not
 9 *enjoined* joined
10 *chevalier* a lady's cavalier or gallant
11 'always aiming at the most outstanding achievements in honour of his glorious
    cause' (the love for Bel-imperia that inspired him).
16 *Nemesis* the goddess of retribution, especially as exercised by the gods against
    human presumption
17 *Envying at* regarding with ill-will
19–20 Kyd probably refers to *Aeneid*, II, ll. 615–16, as Boas suggests, but though
    Pallas (Athene) is there mentioned, it is Juno who is 'ferro accincta', 'girt with
    steel'.
20 *Pallas* Athene, patroness of Athens, and one of the divinities associated with the
    Greeks at Troy
20 *Pergamus* Troy

Brought in a fresh supply of halberdiers,
Which paunched his horse, and dinged him to the ground.
Then young Don Balthazar with ruthless rage,
Taking advantage of his foe's distress,
Did finish what his halberdiers begun,   25
And left not till Andrea's life was done.
Then, though too late, incensed with just remorse,
I with my band set forth against the prince,
And brought him prisoner from his halberdiers.

BEL-IMPERIA
Would thou hadst slain him that so slew my love.   30
But then was Don Andrea's carcase lost?

HORATIO
No, that was it for which I chiefly strove,
Nor stepped I back till I recovered him:
I took him up, and wound him in mine arms,
And welding him unto my private tent,   35
There laid him down, and dewed him with my tears,
And sighed and sorrowed as became a friend.
But neither friendly sorrow, sighs nor tears
Could win pale Death from his unsurpéd right.
Yet this I did, and less I could not do: 40
I saw him honoured with due funeral.
This scarf I plucked from off his lifeless arm,
And wear it in remembrance of my friend.

BEL-IMPERIA
I know the scarf, would he had kept it still,

---

21 *halberdiers* soldiers carrying halberds, weapons that are a combination of spear
   and battle-axe, the head being mounted on a long pole
21-6 Andrea is overwhelmed by superior numbers, not killed in fair combat (see
   Bel-imperia's comment, ll. 73-5). *I Hieronimo* also lays stress on the
   dishonourable way Balthazar brought about Andrea's death (scene xi; and see
   Cairncross, pp. xviii and 49).
22 *paunched* stabbed in the belly
22 *dinged* thrust, struck
27 *just remorse* righteous indignation and pity
34 *wound* embraced
35 *welding* carrying
42 *This scarf* 'Scarves' or 'handkerchers' and sometimes gloves were worn as ladies'
   favours (see l. 47) by knights on the battlefield (compare the 'pledges' Troilus
   and Cressida exchange: *see TC*, IV, iv and V, ii). When Horatio wears the scarf
   (see ll. 48, 49) he becomes visually Andrea's representative; if this scarf is the
   'bloody handkercher' that Hieronimo takes from the dead Horatio's body (see
   II, v, 51 and III, xiii, 86-9) then it also serves as a visual link between the twin
   revenges, for Andrea and Horatio.
42 *lifeless* ed. (liveless *1592*)

For had he lived he would have kept it still,   45
And worn it for his Bel-imperia's sake:
For 'twas my favour at his last depart.
But now wear thou it both for him and me,
For after him thou hast deserved it best.
But, for thy kindness in his life and death,   50
Be sure while Bel-imperia's life endures,
She will be Don Horatio's thankful friend.

HORATIO
And, madam, Don Horatio will not slack
Humbly to serve fair Bel-imperia.
But now, if your good liking stand thereto,   55
I'll crave your pardon to go seek the prince,
For so the duke your father gave me charge.   *Exit*

BEL-IMPERIA
Ay, go Horatio, leave me here alone,
For solitude best fits my cheerless mood.
Yet what avails to wail Andrea's death,   60
From whence Horatio proves my second love?
Had he not loved Andrea as he did,
He could not sit in Bel-imperia's thoughts.
But how can love find harbour in my breast,
Till I revenge the death of my beloved?   65
Yes, second love shall further my revenge.
I'll love Horatio, my Andrea's friend,
The more to spite the prince that wrought his end.
And where Don Balthazar, that slew my love,
Himself now pleads for favour at my hands,   70
He shall in rigour of my just disdain
Reap long repentance for his murderous deed.
For what was't else but murderous cowardice,
So many to oppress one valiant knight,
Without respect of honour in the fight?   75
And here he comes that murdered my delight.

Enter LORENZO *and* BALTHAZAR

47 *favour* a gift given to a lover to be worn as a token of affection
60–8 Bel-imperia's love for Horatio may strike us as sudden, unmotivated and
   even (ll. 66–8) unpleasantly mixed with calculation. Partly this is a matter of
   dramatic convention (the early plays were not greatly concerned with
   psychological probability) and partly an item in Kyd's developing portrait of
   Bel-imperia as a formidable woman, decisively able to control and direct her
   emotions. Her decision is also of course vital in joining the two revenges.
71 *disdain* indignation (*O.E.D.*, sb. 2)
74 *oppress* overwhelm with numbers (*O.E.D.*, 1b)

LORENZO
  Sister, what means this melancholy walk?
BEL-IMPERIA
  That for a while I wish no company.
LORENZO
  But here the prince is come to visit you.
BEL-IMPERIA
  That argues that he lives in liberty.   80
BALTHAZAR
  No madam, but in pleasing servitude.
BEL-IMPERIA
  Your prison then belike is your conceit.
BALTHAZAR
  Ay, by conceit my freedom is enthralled.
BEL-IMPERIA
  Then with conceit enlarge yourself again.
BALTHAZAR
  What if conceit have laid my heart to gage?   85
BEL-IMPERIA
  Pay that you borrowed and recover it.
BALTHAZAR
  I die if it return from whence it lies.
BEL-IMPERIA
  A heartless man, and live? A miracle!
BALTHAZAR
  Ay lady, love can work such miracles.
LORENZO
  Tush, tush, my lord, let go these ambages,   90
  And in plain terms acquaint her with your love.
BEL-IMPERIA
  What boots complaint, when there's no remedy?
BALTHAZAR
  Yes, to your gracious self must I complain,
  In whose fair answer lies my remedy,
  On whose perfection all my thoughts attend,   95

77–89 This stichomythia or line-by-line dialogue is a dramatic convention deriving
    from Seneca. For a reference to Kyd's impressive use of the convention see
    Introduction, pp. xxix–xxx.
82 *conceit* fancy, imagination
83 *enthralled* enslaved
84 *enlarge* set free
85 *laid . . . to gage* given as a pledge, placed in pawn
90 *ambages* oblique, roundabout ways of speaking
92 *What boots complaint* What point is there in pleading your love?

On whose aspect mine eyes find beauty's bower,
In whose translucent breast my heart is lodged.

BEL-IMPERIA
Alas, my lord, these are but words of course,
And but device to drive me from this place.

She, in going in, lets fall her glove, which HORATIO, *coming out, takes up*

HORATIO
Madam, your glove.   100

BEL-IMPERIA
Thanks good Horatio, take it for thy pains.

BALTHAZAR
Signior Horatio stooped in happy time.

HORATIO
I reaped more grace than I deserved or hoped.

LORENZO
My lord, be not dismayed for what is passed,
You know that women oft are humorous: 105
These clouds will overblow with little wind;
Let me alone, I'll scatter them myself.
Meanwhile let us devise to spend the time
In some delightful sports and revelling.

HORATIO
The king, my lords, is coming hither straight,   110
To feast the Portingale ambassador:
Things were in readiness before I came.

BALTHAZAR
Then here it fits us to attend the king,
To welcome hither our ambassador,
And learn my father and my country's health.   115

Enter the Banquet, Trumpets, *the* KING, *and* AMBASSADOR

96 *aspect* form, appearance
98 *words of course* conventional phrases
99 *device* ed. (deuise *1592*)
99 s.d. This rather awkward piece of stage-action may be intended to underline the part accident plays in the linked process of 'revenge'. Compare the direction 'a letter falleth' (III, ii, 23) and the letter written by Pedringano which finds its way by chance into Hieronimo's hands at III, vii, 19 ff.
105 *humorous* temperamental
113 *fits* befits
115 s.d. *the Banquet, Trumpets* Another opportunity for display, underlining the proud, self-confident society of the Spanish court. A full-scale occasion is evidently intended (not just a buffet-type banquet often used on the Elizabethan stage) for they 'sit to the banquet' (l. 127 s.d.) and remain seated to watch Hieronimo's entertainment.

KING
  See Lord Ambassador, how Spain entreats
  Their prisoner Balthazar, thy viceroy's son:
  We pleasure more in kindness than in wars.
AMBASSADOR
  Sad is our king, and Portingale laments,
  Supposing that Don Balthazar is slain.   120
BALTHAZAR
  [*Aside*] So am I slain by beauty's tyranny.
  [*To him*] You see, my lord, how Balthazar is slain:
  I frolic with the Duke of Castile's son,
  Wrapped every hour in pleasures of the court,
  And graced with favours of his majesty.   125
KING
  Put off your greetings till our feast be done;
  Now come and sit with us and taste our cheer.
                        [*They*] *sit to the banquet*
  Sit down young prince, you are our second guest;
  Brother sit down and nephew take your place;
  Signior Horatio, wait thou upon our cup,   130
  For well thou hast deserved to be honoured.
  Now, lordings, fall to; Spain is Portugal,
  And Portugal is Spain, we both are friends,
  Tribute is paid, and we enjoy our right.
  But where is old Hieronimo, our marshal?   135
  He promised us, in honour of our guest,
  To grace our banquet with some pompous jest.

Enter HIERONIMO *with a* Drum, *three* KNIGHTS, *each* [*with*] *his*
scutcheon: then he fetches three KINGS, [*the* KNIGHTS] *take their*
crowns and them captive

118 *pleasure* take pleasure
121 This aside hints the trouble that is breeding under the surface appearance of
     order.
135 ff. Hieronimo's entertainment appeals to English patriotism at a moment (the
     1580s or very early 1590s) when Spain was the arch-enemy; theatre-goers
     would have expected some patriotic flourish. The history is popular rather than
     scholarly; for a full discussion of Kyd's sources and of his errors concerning the
     earls of Gloucester and Kent and the duke of Lancaster see Boas, pp. 397–8,
     Edwards, p. 26 fn. and Freeman, pp. 55 ff. Hill (p. 160) takes it that the King's
     remarks at ll. 147–50 and 158–60 would be understood as absurdly beside the
     point by a theatre audience alert to the patriotic implications of the dumb-
     shows
137 *pompous jest* stately entertainment
137 s.d. *Drum* a drummer
137 s.d. *scutcheon* shield with armorial bearings

Hieronimo, this masque contents mine eye,
Although I sound not well the mystery.
HIERONIMO
The first armed knight, that hung his scutcheon up,   140
     He takes the scutcheon and gives it to the KING
Was English Robert, Earl of Gloucester,
Who when King Stephen bore sway in Albion,
Arrived with five and twenty thousand men
In Portingale, and by success of war
Enforced the king, then but a Saracen,   145
To bear the yoke of the English monarchy.
KING
My lord of Portingale, by this you see
That which may comfort both your king and you,
And make your late discomfort seem the less.
But say, Hieronimo, what was the next?   150
HIERONIMO
The second knight, that hung his scutcheon up,
     He doth as he did before
Was Edmund, Earl of Kent in Albion,
When English Richard wore the diadem;
He came likewise, and razed Lisbon walls,
And took the King of Portingale in fight: 155
For which, and other suchlike service done,
He after was created Duke of York.
KING
This is another special argument,
That Portingale may deign to bear our yoke,
When it by little England hath been yoked.   160
But now Hieronimo, what were the last?
HIERONIMO
The third and last, not least in our account,
     Doing as before
Was as the rest a valiant Englishman,
Brave John of Gaunt, the Duke of Lancaster,
As by his scutcheon plainly may appear.   165
He with a puissant army came to Spain,
And took our King of Castile prisoner.

---

139 *sound* understand, fathom
139 *mystery* significance, hidden meaning
142 *Albion* England
158 *special* particular, appropriate (*O.E.D.*, 5)
158 *argument* illustration, proof
166 *puissant* powerful

AMBASSADOR

  This is an argument for our viceroy,
  That Spain may not insult for her success,
  Since English warriors likewise conquered Spain,   170
  And made them bow their knees to Albion.

KING

  Hieronimo, I drink to thee for this device,
  Which hath pleased both the ambassador and me;
  Pledge me Hieronimo, if thou love the king.
                        Takes the cup of HORATIO
  My lord, I fear we sit but over-long,   175
  Unless our dainties were more delicate:
  But welcome are you to the best we have.
  Now let us in, that you may be despatched,
  I think our council is already set.
                               Exeunt omnes

Act I, Scene v

ANDREA

  Come we for this from depth of underground,
  To see him feast that gave me my death's wound?
  These pleasant sights are sorrow to my soul,
  Nothing but league, and love, and banqueting!

REVENGE

  Be still Andrea, ere we go from hence,   5
  I'll turn their friendship into fell despite,
  Their love to mortal hate, their day to night,
  Their hope into despair, their peace to war,
  Their joys to pain, their bliss to misery.

---

169 *insult* boast
172 *device* show, masque (see l. 138)
174 s.d. *of* from
176 *Unless* unless it were that
  1–2 Andrea's complaint echoes a Senecan tragic motif, the complaint of returning
  ghosts that what they see is contrary to their wishes.
  1 ff. The Andrea – Revenge exchange serves to maintain the audience's sense of
  ironv: Revenge plays up (ll. 6 ff.) the antitheses of love and hate, hope and
  despair, bliss and misery that underlie it.
  6 *fell despite* cruel hatred

Act II, Scene i

Enter LORENZO *and* BALTHAZAR

LORENZO

My lord, though Bel-imperia seem thus coy,
Let reason hold you in your wonted joy:
'In time the savage bull sustains the yoke,
In time all haggard hawks will stoop to lure,
In time small wedges cleave the hardest oak,   5
In time the flint is pierced with softest shower' –
And she in time will fall from her disdain,
And rue the sufferance of your friendly pain.

BALTHAZAR

'No, she is wilder, and more hard withal,
Than beast, or bird, or tree, or stony wall'.   10
But wherefore blot I Bel-imperia's name?
It is my fault, not she, that merits blame.
My feature is not to content her sight,
My words are rude and work her no delight.

1 *coy* disdainful, unresponsive

3 *sustains* undergoes, has to submit to (*O.E.D.*, 9)

3–6 Lorenzo argues in the sonneteering vein extremely popular at this date,
quoting, almost word for word, a sonnet in Thomas Watson's *Hecatompathia*
(entered for publication 1582). The lines represent conventional notions about
the courtship of reluctant ladies, and therefore deliberately adopt the artifices of
up-to-date poetry on the subject. Line 3 is recalled in *Much Ado* (I, i, 258) as
Don Pedro prophesies that even Benedick will fall victim to love.

4 *haggard* wild, untrained

4 *stoop to lure* swoop down to the lure, a dead bird, or feathers made to resemble a
bird, used for training hawks

5 *wedges* wedge-shaped pieces of metal used in felling trees

8 *rue* pity

8 *sufferance* patient endurance

9–10 Balthazar quotes (with variation) the lines of Watson's sonnet that follow
those quoted by Lorenzo. (The original reads: 'More fierce is my sweet loue,
more hard withall,/Then Beast, or Birde, then Tree, or Stony wall.') The two
young men are showing their familiarity with contemporary poetry.

11–18 Balthazar's speech became famous, and was often parodied. The parodists,
like modern readers, are no doubt reacting against this highly artificial and self-
conscious way of dramatising indecision and self-doubt. Balthazar must of
course be at least half-ridiculous here, being excessively in love, and being in
any case a weak nature.

13 *feature* form, bearing (not merely the face)   13 *to* such as to

The lines I send her are but harsh and ill,   15
Such as do drop from Pan and Marsyas' quill.
My presents are not of sufficient cost,
And being worthless all my labour's lost.
Yet might she love me for my valiancy;
Ay, but that's slandered by captivity.   20
Yet might she love me to content her sire;
Ay, but her reason masters his desire.
Yet might she love me as her brother's friend;
Ay, but her hopes aim at some other end.
Yet might she love me to uprear her state;   25
Ay, but perhaps she hopes some nobler mate.
Yet might she love me as her beauty's thrall;
Ay, but I fear she cannot love at all.

LORENZO
My lord, for my sake leave these ecstasies,
And doubt not but we'll find some remedy.   30
Some cause there is that lets you not be loved:
First that must needs be known, and then removed.
What if my sister love some other knight?

BALTHAZAR
My summer's day will turn to winter's night.

LORENZO
I have already found a stratagem,   35
To sound the bottom of this doubtful theme.
My lord, for once you shall be ruled by me:
Hinder me not whate'er you hear or see.
By force or fair means will I cast about
To find the truth of all this question out.   40
Ho, Pedringano!

PEDRINGANO   [*Within*] Signior!
LORENZO   *Vien qui presto.*

---

16 *Pan and Marsyas* Each of these gods, in different stories, challenged Apollo to
contests in flute-playing; neither could match his skill and both were punished.
16 *quill* either a musical pipe or a pen; Kyd appears to use both senses here.
19 *valiancy* valour
20 *slandered* brought into disrepute (*O.E.D.*, v, 2)
25 *uprear her state* improve her social position
27 *beauty's* ed. (beauteous *1592*)
29 *ecstasies* unreasoning passions (Edwards). Lorenzo's word shows that Kyd
meant Balthazar's speech to be delivered in an exaggerated fashion.
36 *sound the bottom* discover the exact features (the metaphor is from 'sounding' a
waterway to detect snags and shallows)
41 *Vien qui presto* Come here quickly (Italian)   41 *qui* ed. (*que 1592*)

Enter PEDRINGANO

PEDRINGANO
  Hath your lordship any service to command me?
LORENZO
  Ay, Pedringano, service of import.
  And not to spend the time in trifling words,
  Thus stands the case: it is not long thou know'st,   45
  Since I did shield thee from my father's wrath,
  For thy conveyance in Andrea's love,
  For which thou wert adjudged to punishment.
  I stood betwixt thee and thy punishment;
  And since, thou know'st how I have favoured thee.   50
  Now to these favours will I add reward,
  Not with fair words, but store of golden coin,
  And lands and living joined with dignities,
  If thou but satisfy my just demand.
  Tell truth and have me for thy lasting friend.   55
PEDRINGANO
  Whate'er it be your lordship shall demand,
  My bounden duty bids me tell the truth,
  If case it lie in me to tell the truth.
LORENZO
  Then, Pedringano, this is my demand:
  Whom loves my sister Bel-imperia?   60
  For she reposeth all her trust in thee –
  Speak man, and gain both friendship and reward:
  I mean, whom loves she in Andrea's place?
PEDRINGANO
  Alas, my lord, since Don Andrea's death,
  I have no credit with her as before,   65
  And therefore know not if she love or no.
LORENZO
  Nay, if thou dally then I am thy foe,   [*Draws his sword*]
  And fear shall force what friendship cannot win.
  Thy death shall bury what thy life conceals.
  Thou diest for more esteeming her than me.   70
PEDRINGANO
  O, stay, my lord.

---

47 *conveyance* secret or underhand dealing
52 *store* abundance
58 *it lie in me* I am able to
71 *stay* wait, hold off

LORENZO
  Yet speak the truth and I will guerdon thee,
  And shield thee from whatever can ensue,
  And will conceal whate'er proceeds from thee:
  But if thou dally once again, thou diest.   75
PEDRINGANO
  If Madam Bel-imperia be in love –
LORENZO
  What, villain, ifs and ands?   [*Offers to kill him*]
PEDRINGANO
  O stay my lord, she loves Horatio.

                                        BALTHAZAR *starts back*

LORENZO
  What, Don Horatio our Knight Marshal's son?
PEDRINGANO
  Even him my lord.   80
LORENZO
  Now say but how know'st thou he is her love,
  And thou shalt find me kind and liberal:
  Stand up, I say, and fearless tell the truth.
PEDRINGANO
  She sent him letters which myself perused,
  Full-fraught with lines and arguments of love,   85
  Preferring him before Prince Balthazar.
LORENZO
  Swear on this cross that what thou say'st is true,
  And that thou wilt conceal what thou hast told.
PEDRINGANO
  I swear to both by him that made us all.
LORENZO
  In hope thine oath is true, here's thy reward,   90
  But if I prove thee perjured and unjust,
  This very sword whereon thou took'st thine oath,
  Shall be the worker of thy tragedy.

72 *guerdon* reward
77 *ifs and ands* 'ifs and ifs' ('and' used to mean 'if'). A strong theatrical moment
   (as Lorenzo lunges at Pedringano) that Nashe may be remembering in his
   preface to Greene's *Menaphon*, where he writes of 'translators' who are content
   'to bodge up a blank verse with ifs and ands'.
85 *fraught* loaded
87 *this cross* his sword-hilt
90 *In hope* in the faith that
91 *unjust* false, dishonest

PEDRINGANO

    What I have said is true, and shall for me
    Be still concealed from Bel-imperia.   95
    Besides, your honour's liberality
    Deserves my duteous service even till death.

LORENZO

    Let this be all that thou shalt do for me:
    Be watchful when, and where, these lovers meet,
    And give me notice in some secret sort.   100

PEDRINGANO

    I will my lord.

LORENZO

    Then shalt thou find that I am liberal.
    Thou know'st that I can more advance thy state
    Than she, be therefore wise and fail me not.
    Go and attend her as thy custom is,   105
    Lest absence make her think thou dost amiss.

                                Exit PEDRINGANO

    Why so: *tam armis quam ingenio:*
    Where words prevail not, violence prevails;
    But gold doth more than either of them both.
    How likes Prince Balthazar this stratagem?   110

BALTHAZAR

    Both well, and ill: it makes me glad and sad:
    Glad, that I know the hinderer of my love,
    Sad, that I fear she hates me whom I love.
    Glad, that I know on whom to be revenged,
    Sad, that she'll fly me if I take revenge.   115
    Yet must I take revenge or die myself,
    For love resisted grows impatient.
    I think Horatio be my destined plague:
    First, in his hand he brandished a sword,
    And with that sword he fiercely waged war,   120

---

100 *in some secret sort* by some secret means
103 *advance thy state* improve your social position and your finances
107 *tam . . . ingenio* by equal parts of force and skill
111–33 Clemen (pp. 106–7) usefully comments: 'the lack of substance in this
    repetitive style of his, tediously amplified by antithesis and other rhetorical
    figures, is exactly in keeping with the irresolute, dependent, puppet-like role
    that Balthazar is to sustain in the play.' His speech here parallels and
    complements his lines on Bel-imperia (ll. 9 ff.) near the scene's beginning.

And in that war he gave me dangerous wounds,
And by those wounds he forced me to yield,
And by my yielding I became his slave.
Now in his mouth he carries pleasing words,
Which pleasing words do harbour sweet conceits,   125
Which sweet conceits are limed with sly deceits,
Which sly deceits smooth Bel-imperia's ears,
And through her ears dive down into her heart,
And in her heart set him where I should stand.
Thus hath he ta'en my body by his force,   130
And now by sleight would captivate my soul:
But in his fall I'll tempt the destinies,
And either lose my life, or win my love.

LORENZO
Let's go, my lord, your staying stays revenge.
Do you but follow me and gain your love: 135
Her favour must be won by his remove.   *Exeunt*

Act II, Scene ii

Enter HORATIO *and* BEL-IMPERIA

HORATIO
Now, madam, since by favour of your love
Our hidden smoke is turned to open flame,
And that with looks and words we feed our thoughts
(Two chief contents, where more cannot be had),

---

125 *sweet conceits* pleasing figures of speech
126 *limed with* made into traps with (from bird-lime, a gluey substance used to catch birds)
127 *smooth* seduce, flatter (compare *O.E.D.*, v, 5a)
131 *sleight* trickery
132 *in his fall* in causing his downfall
  3 *thoughts* ed. (though *1592*) wishes, imaginings
  4 *contents* sources of contentment

Thus in the midst of love's fair blandishments,   5
Why show you sign of inward languishments?

PEDRINGANO *showeth all to the* PRINCE *and* LORENZO,
                                placing them in secret [*above*]

BEL-IMPERIA
My heart, sweet friend, is like a ship at sea:
She wisheth port, where riding all at ease,
She may repair what stormy times have worn,
And leaning on the shore, may sing with joy   10
That pleasure follows pain, and bliss annoy.
Possession of thy love is th'only port,
Wherein my heart, with fears and hopes long tossed,
Each hour doth wish and long to make resort;
There to repair the joys that it hath lost,   15
And sitting safe, to sing in Cupid's choir
That sweetest bliss is crown of love's desire.

BALTHAZAR
O sleep mine eyes, see not my love profaned;
Be deaf, my ears, hear not my discontent;
Die, heart, another joys what thou deservest.   20

LORENZO
Watch still mine eyes, to see this love disjoined;
Hear still mine ears, to hear them both lament;
Live, heart, to joy at fond Horatio's fall.

6 s.d. Balthazar and Lorenzo watch the lovers from the upper-stage or balcony.
    Edwards is, I think, correct in arguing that *1592*'s 'Balthazar aboue', after l. 17
    is an author's clarification; like him I transfer the 'above' to the end of the
    present direction.
7 *friend* love (a common Elizabethan sense)
9 *may* ed. (mad 1592)
15 *repair* restore
16 *sing* celebrate
17 *is* which is
17 *1592* has s.d. '*Balthazar* above'; Edwards suggests, convincingly, that this is a
    note by the author to clarify the earlier direction (1. 6) and need not be repeated.
18 ff. The antithetical speeches by the lovers and those watching them is one of
    Kyd's more obvious ways of insisting on dramatic irony. Bel-imperia's
    description of the bower (ll. 42 ff.) is also obviously and grimly ironic.
20 *joys* enjoys
23 *fond* foolish, besotted

BEL-IMPERIA
    Why stands Horatio speechless all this while?
HORATIO
    The less I speak, the more I meditate.   25
BEL-IMPERIA
    But whereon dost thou chiefly meditate?
HORATIO
    On dangers past, and pleasures to ensue.
BALTHAZAR
    On pleasures past, and dangers to ensue.
BEL-IMPERIA
    What dangers and what pleasures dost thou mean?
HORATIO
    Dangers of war and pleasures of our love.   30
LORENZO
    Dangers of death, but pleasures none at all.
BEL-IMPERIA
    Let dangers go, thy war shall be with me,
    But such a war as breaks no bond of peace.
    Speak thou fair words, I'll cross them with fair words;
    Send thou sweet looks, I'll meet them with sweet looks; 35
    Write loving lines, I'll answer loving lines;
    Give me a kiss, I'll countercheck thy kiss:
    Be this our warring peace, or peaceful war.
HORATIO
    But gracious madam, then appoint the field
    Where trial of this war shall first be made.   40
BALTHAZAR
    Ambitious villain, how his boldness grows!
BEL-IMPERIA
    Then be thy father's pleasant bower the field,
    Where first we vowed a mutual amity:
    The court were dangerous, that place is safe.

---

33 *war* ed. (warring *1592*)
34 *cross* mèet, complement (a punning reference to cross meaning thwart, go
    counter to, is intended)
37 *countercheck* oppose, take countering action against
42 *bower* an arbour, or enclosed garden-seat, covered with branches of trees, plants
    etc. Cf. II, iv, 53 s.d. and note.

Our hour shall be when Vesper gins to rise, 45
That summons home distressful travellers.
There none shall hear us but the harmless birds:
Happily the gentle nightingale
Shall carol us asleep ere we be ware,
And singing with the prickle at her breast, 50
Tell our delight and mirthful dalliance.
Till then each hour will seem a year and more.

HORATIO
But, honey sweet, and honourable love,
Return we now into your father's sight:
Dangerous suspicion waits on our delight. 55

LORENZO
Ay, danger mixed with jealous despite
Shall send thy soul into eternal night. *Exeunt*

Act II, Scene iii

Enter KING *of Spain, Portingale* AMBASSADOR, DON CYPRIAN,
etc.

KING
Brother of Castile, to the prince's love
What says your daughter Bel-imperia?

CASTILE
Although she coy it as becomes her kind,
And yet dissemble that she loves the prince,
I doubt not, I, but she will stoop in time. 5
And were she froward, which she will not be,
Yet herein shall she follow my advice,
Which is to love him or forgo my love.

KING
Then, Lord Ambassador of Portingale,

45 *Vesper* the evening star or Venus
46 *distressful travellers* weary labourers ('travel' and 'travail' were closely linked in Elizabethan use)
48 *Happily* haply, perhaps
50 *prickle* thorn
56 *jealous* ed. (jealous *1592*) watchful, suspicious; metre requires three syllables
3 *coy it* affects disinclination
3 *as becomes her kind* as it is a woman's nature to do
5 *stoop* become obedient; and compare II, i, 4 and note.
6 *froward* perverse, refractory

Advise thy king to make this marriage up,   10
For strengthening of our late-confirmed league;
I know no better means to make us friends.
Her dowry shall be large and liberal:
Besides that she is daughter and half-heir
Unto our brother here, Don Cyprian,   15
And shall enjoy the moiety of his land,
I'll grace her marriage with an uncle's gift.
And this it is: in case the match go forward,
The tribute which you pay shall be released,
And if by Balthazar she have a son,   20
He shall enjoy the kingdom after us.

AMBASSADOR
I'll make the motion to my sovereign liege,
And work it if my counsel may prevail.

KING
Do so, my lord, and if he give consent,
I hope his presence here will honour us   25
In celebration of the nuptial day –
And let himself determine of the time.

AMBASSADOR
Will't please your grace command me aught beside?

KING
Commend me to the king, and so farewell.
But where's Prince Balthazar to take his leave?   30

AMBASSADOR
That is performed already, my good lord.

KING
Amongst the rest of what you have in charge,
The prince's ransom must not be forgot;
That's none of mine, but his that took him prisoner,
And well his forwardness deserves reward: 35
It was Horatio, our Knight Marshal's son.

AMBASSADOR
Between us there's a price already pitched,
And shall be sent with all convenient speed.

KING
Then once again farewell, my lord.

AMBASSADOR
Farewell, my Lord of Castile and the rest.   *Exit*   40

16 *moiety* a half-share
22 *make the motion* put the proposal
35 *forwardness* enterprise, zeal
37 *pitched* agreed

KING
    Now, brother, you must take some little pains
    To win fair Bel-imperia from her will:
    Young virgins must be ruled by their friends.
    The prince is amiable, and loves her well,
    If she neglect him and forgo his love,   45
    She both will wrong her own estate and ours.
    Therefore, whiles I do entertain the prince
    With greatest pleasure that our court affords,
    Endeavour you to win your daughter's thought:
    If she give back, all this will come to naught.   *Exeunt*   50

Act II, Scene iv

Enter HORATIO, BEL-IMPERIA, *and* PEDRINGANO

HORATIO
    Now that the night begins with sable wings
    To overcloud the brightness of the sun,
    And that in darkness pleasures may be done,
    Come Bel-imperia, let us to the bower,
    And there in safety pass a pleasant hour.   5
BEL-IMPERIA
    I follow thee my love, and will not back,
    Although my fainting heart controls my soul.
HORATIO
    Why, make you doubt of Pedringano's faith?
BEL-IMPERIA
    No, he is as trusty as my second self.
    Go Pedringano, watch without the gate,   10
    And let us know if any make approach.
PEDRINGANO
    [*Aside*] Instead of watching, I'll deserve more gold

---

42 *will* wilfulness
49 *thought* ed. (thoughts *1592*)
50 *give back* 'turn her back on us' (Edwards), refuse
 1 *sable* black
 1-5 An Elizabethan audience would immediately feel the irony of invoking night, associated with evil, to watch over the relationship. The ironies are strengthened in the next lines; see esp. ll. 16-19.
 7 *controls* oppresses, masters (the heart's fearfulness struggles against the soul's wishes)
10 *without* outside

By fetching Don Lorenzo to this match.

                                   Exit PEDRINGANO

HORATIO

  What means my love?

BEL-IMPERIA   I know not what myself.

  And yet my heart foretells me some mischance.   15

HORATIO

  Sweet say not so, fair fortune is our friend,

  And heavens have shut up day to pleasure us.

  The stars thou see'st hold back their twinkling shine,

  And Luna hides herself to pleasure us.

BEL-IMPERIA

  Thou hast prevailed, I'll conquer my misdoubt,   20

  And in thy love and counsel drown my fear.

  I fear no more, love now is all my thoughts.

  Why sit we not? for pleasure asketh ease.

HORATIO

  The more thou sit'st within these leafy bowers,

  The more will Flora deck it with her flowers.   25

BEL-IMPERIA

  Ay, but if Flora spy Horatio here,

  Her jealous eye will think I sit too near.

HORATIO

  Hark, madam, how the birds record by night,

  For joy that Bel-imperia sits in sight.

BEL-IMPERIA

  No, Cupid counterfeits the nightingale,   30

  To frame sweet music to Horatio's tale.

HORATIO

  If Cupid sing, then Venus is not far:

  Ay, thou art Venus or some fairer star.

BEL-IMPERIA

  If I be Venus, thou must needs be Mars,

  And where Mars reigneth, there must needs be wars.   35

HORATIO

  Then thus begin our wars: put forth thy hand,

---

13 *match* meeting

19 *Luna* the moon

23 *asketh* needs, requires

28 *record* sing

31 *frame* adapt, compose

32-5 *Venus ... Mars* Aphrodite (Venus) was unfaithful to her husband Hephaestus with Ares (Mars) the god of war.

35 *wars* ed. (war *1592*); rhyme requires the plural form

That it may combat with my ruder hand.
BEL-IMPERIA
Set forth thy foot to try the push of mine.
HORATIO
But first my looks shall combat against thine.
BEL-IMPERIA
Then ward thyself: I dart this kiss at thee.   40
HORATIO
Thus I retort the dart thou threw'st at me.
BEL-IMPERIA
Nay then, to gain the glory of the field,
My twining arms shall yoke and make thee yield.
HORATIO
Nay then, my arms are large and strong withal:
Thus elms by vines are compassed till they fall.   45
BEL-IMPERIA
O let me go, for in my troubled eyes
Now may'st thou read that life in passion dies.
HORATIO
O stay a while and I will die with thee,
So shalt thou yield and yet have conquered me.
BEL-IMPERIA
Who's there? Pedringano! We are betrayed!   50

Enter LORENZO, BALTHAZAR, SERBERINE, PEDRINGANO,
disguised

LORENZO
My lord, away with her, take her aside.
O sir, forbear, your valour is already tried.

37 *ruder* rougher, coarser
40 *ward* guard, shield
42-7 Bercovitch (pp. 223-4) comments on the tense opposition of the Empedoclean principles of love and strife here. Entwined elms and vines are the
traditional symbols of Venus, but here the vines cause the 'fall' of the elms.
43-5 Edwards shows that Horatio here inverts a familiar saying about the elm
(usually an emblem of friendship: the vine holds up the tree in its embraces);
taken with the double meaning in 'die' (a common sexual pun), it becomes
obvious that Kyd wishes to emphasise the sensuality of the moment, thus
making the ironies more emotionally charged. The literal sense of l. 48 does of
course come about; a somewhat heavy-handed irony.
44 *withal* ed. (with *1592*)
50 *Who's there? Pedringano!* ed. (Whose there *Pedringano? 1592*)
52 *tried* tested, proved. The thought of Horatio's martial prowess still rankles with
Lorenzo.

Quickly despatch, my masters.

They hang him in the arbour

HORATIO

What, will you murder me?

LORENZO

Ay, thus, and thus; these are the fruits of love.   55

They stab him

BEL-IMPERIA

O save his life and let me die for him!
O save him, brother, save him, Balthazar:
I loved Horatio, but he loved not me.

BALTHAZAR

But Balthazar loves Bel-imperia.

LORENZO

Although his life were still ambitious proud,   60
Yet is he at the highest now he is dead.

BEL-IMPERIA

Murder! murder! Help, Hieronimo, help!

LORENZO

Come, stop her mouth, away with her.

Exeunt [, leaving HORATIO's *body]*

Act II, Scene v

Enter HIERONIMO *in his shirt, etc.*

HIERONIMO

What outcries pluck me from my naked bed,
And chill my throbbing heart with trembling fear,
Which never danger yet could daunt before?
Who calls Hieronimo? Speak, here I am.

53 s.d. Whether a stage-tree was used for this purpose remains unclear; Isabella
(IV, ii, 6 ff.) seems to refer to a tree; Hieronimo says (IV, iv, 111) he found
Horatio 'hanging on a tree'; the author of the Fourth Addition thinks very
specifically of a tree (see ll. 60 ff.). But editors may well be right in arguing that
the arbour illustrated on the title-page of the 1615 edition (a trellis-work arch
with a seat in it) may have been decorated with leaves and branches, and so have
served as both arbour and tree.

60 *ambitious proud* ambitious for a position that would satisfy his pride

1 s.d. *shirt* nightshirt. For a description of probable stage-practice here see Fourth
Addition ll. 135–9.

1 *naked bed* a transferred epithet; the sleeper is naked (or lightly clothed).
Edwards says the phrase was familiar.

1–33 Hieronimo's soliloquy, perhaps the most famous of the play, is one which, as
Clemen (p. 102) points out, 'is not only spoken but acted', carrying its own
internal 'stage-directions', a technique followed, and made more subtle, by
Shakespeare.

I did not slumber, therefore 'twas no dream,   5
No, no, it was some woman cried for help,
And here within this garden did she cry,
And in this garden must I rescue her.
But stay, what murderous spectacle is this?
A man hanged up and all the murderers gone,   10
And in my bower to lay the guilt on me.
This place was made for pleasure not for death.

He cuts him down

Those garments that he wears I oft have seen –
Alas, it is Horatio, my sweet son!
Oh no, but he that whilom was my son.   15
O was it thou that calledst me from my bed?
O speak, if any spark of life remain:
I am thy father. Who hath slain my son?
What savage monster, not of human kind,
Hath here been glutted with thy harmless blood,   20
And left thy bloody corpse dishonoured here,
For me, amidst this dark and deathful shades,
To drown thee with an ocean of my tears?
O heavens, why made you night to cover sin?
By day this deed of darkness had not been.   25
O earth, why didst thou not in time devour
The vild profaner of this sacred bower?
O poor Horatio, what hadst thou misdone,
To leese thy life ere life was new begun?
O wicked butcher, whatsoe'er thou wert,   30
How could thou strangle virtue and desert?
Ay me most wretched, that have lost my joy,
In leesing my Horatio, my sweet boy!

Enter ISABELLA

ISABELLA
My husband's absence makes my heart to throb –
Hieronimo!   35

---

12 continuing the pleasure/death irony of II, ii and II, iv
13 ff. Good direction and acting can make the moment of discovery deeply
   poignant. Kyd's words may seem absurdly simple here, but he is surely right not
   to overload Hieronimo's speech with rhetoric.
15 *whilom* in the past, till now
22 *this* an accepted plural form at this date
26 *in time* at the due moment
27 *vild* vile   29 *leese* lose
29 *was new begun* had entered a new phase; perhaps the reference is to Horatio's
   new life as a prominent citizen after his success in war

HIERONIMO

Here, Isabella, help me to lament,
For sighs are stopped and all my tears are spent.

ISABELLA

What world of grief! My son Horatio!
O where's the author of this endless woe?

HIERONIMO

To know the author were some ease of grief,   40
For in revenge my heart would find relief.

ISABELLA

Then is he gone? and is my son gone too?
O, gush out, tears, fountains and floods of tears;
Blow, sighs, and raise an everlasting storm:
For outrage fits our cursed wretchedness.   45

HIERONIMO

Sweet lovely rose, ill plucked before thy time,
Fair worthy son, not conquered, but betrayed:
I'll kiss thee now, for words with tears are stayed.

ISABELLA

And I'll close up the glasses of his sight,
For once these eyes were only my delight.   50

HIERONIMO

See'st thou this handkercher besmeared with blood?
It shall not from me till I take revenge.
See'st thou those wounds that yet are bleeding fresh?
I'll not entomb them till I have revenged.
Then will I joy amidst my discontent,   55
Till then my sorrow never shall be spent.

ISABELLA

The heavens are just, murder cannot be hid:
Time is the author both of truth and right,
And time will bring this treachery to light.

39 *author* the one responsible
45 *outrage* passionate behaviour (*O.E.D.*, sb. 2)
48 *with* by
48 *stayed* ed. (stainde *1592*) stopped
49 *glasses of his sight* his eyes
51 *handkercher* handkerchief, small scarf
51-2 For the possible origin of this 'handkercher' see I, iv, 42 note.
57-9 Isabella's words are a common Elizabethan axiom (see Tilley M1315),
    skilfully used by Kyd to contrast with Hieronimo's complete bewilderment.
    Broude regards Isabella's summary of the Veritas Filia Temporis *topos* (l. 58) as
    a succinct expression of the uniting theme of the play.

HIERONIMO

Meanwhile, good Isabella, cease thy plaints,   60
Or at the least dissemble them awhile:
So shall we sooner find the practice out,
And learn by whom all this was brought about.
Come Isabel, now let us take him up,

They take him up

And bear him in from out this cursed place.   65
I'll say his dirge, singing fits not this case.
O aliquis mihi quas pulchrum ver educat herbas

HIERONIMO *sets his breast unto his sword*

Misceat, et nostro detur medicina dolori;
Aut, si qui faciunt animis oblivia, succos
Praebeat; ipse metam magnum quaecunque per orbem   70
Gramina Sol pulchras effert in luminis oras;
Ipse bibam quicquid meditatur saga veneni,
Quicquid et herbarum vi caeca nenia nectit:
Omnia perpetiar, lethum quoque, dum semel omnis
Noster in extincto moriatur pectore sensus.   75
Ergo tuos oculos nunquam, mea vita, videbo,
Et tua perpetuus sepelivit lumina somnus?
Emoriar tecum: sic, sic juvat ire sub umbras.
At tamen absistam properato cedere letho,
Ne mortem vindicta tuam tum nulla sequatur.   80

Here he throws it from him and bears the body away

60 *plaints* complaints, sorrowing   62 *practice* plot
66 *dirge* funeral song or hymn (from *dirige*, the first word of a Latin antiphon in
the office for the dead)   67 *ver educat* ed. (*var educet 1592*)
67–80 'Let someone bind for me the herbs which beautiful spring fosters, and let a
salve be given for our grief; or let him apply juices, if there are any that bring
forgetfulness to men's minds. I myself shall gather anywhere in the great world
whatever plants the sun draws forth into the fair regions of light; I myself shall
drink whatever drug the wise-woman devises, and whatever herbs incantation
assembles by its secret power. I shall face all things, death even, until the moment
our every feeling dies in this dead breast. And so shall I never again, my life, see
those eyes of yours, and has everlasting slumber sealed up your light of life? I shall
perish with you; thus, thus would it please me to go to the shades below. But none
the less I shall keep myself from yielding to a hastened death, lest in that case no
revenge should follow your death.' The passage, which contains reminiscences of
Lucretius, Virgil and Ovid, is 'a *pastiche*, in Kyd's singular fashion, of tags from
classical poetry, and lines of his own composition' (Boas).
69 *animis oblivia* ed. (*annum oblimia 1592*)
70 *metam magnum quaecunque* ed. (*metum magnam quicunque 1592*)
71 *effert* ed. (*effecit 1592*)   72 *veneni* ed. (*veneri 1592*)
73 *herbarum vi caeca nenia* ed. (*irraui euecaeca menta 1592*)
75 *pectore* ed. (*pectora 1592*)   80 *tum* ed. (*tam 1592*)

Act II, Scene vi

ANDREA
  Brought'st thou me hither to increase my pain?
  I looked that Balthazar should have been slain;
  But 'tis my friend Horatio that is slain,
  And they abuse fair Bel-imperia,
  On whom I doted more than all the world,   5
  Because she loved me more than all the world.
REVENGE
  Thou talk'st of harvest when the corn is green:
  The end is crown of every work well done;
  The sickle comes not till the corn be ripe.
  Be still, and ere I lead thee from this place,   10
  I'll show thee Balthazar in heavy case.

Act III, Scene i

Enter VICEROY *of Portingale*, NOBLES, VILLUPPO

VICEROY
  Infortunate condition of kings,
  Seated amidst so many helpless doubts!
  First we are placed upon extremest height,
  And oft supplanted with exceeding heat,
  But ever subject to the wheel of chance;   5

1 ff. One effect of the Andrea-Revenge exchange is to maintain an audience's
    detachment, threatened by the emotion-laden events of the past scenes.
2 *looked* expected, hoped
5 *On* ed. (Or *1592*)
11 *in heavy case* in a sad state
1 s.d. NOBLES, VILLUPPO ed. (*Nobles, Alexandro, Villuppo 1592*)
1–11 This is a common theme in Elizabethan writing (see e.g. *Richard II*, III, ii,
    155 ff.) and with parallels also in Seneca (see *Agamemnon*, 57–73).
1 *Infortunate* ill-used by Fortune
2 *Seated* placed
2 *helpless* for which there is no help
2 *doubts* fears
4 *heat* fury
5 *the wheel of chance* The common Elizabethan figure to describe the cycle of
    achievement and failure in human (and especially political) life: kings rise to
    the top of the wheel in prosperity and fall, inevitably, to its lowest point in
    defeat and death. See Introduction, p. xxiv for the ironies of this speech and this
    scene.

And at our highest never joy we so,
As we both doubt and dread our overthrow.
So striveth not the waves with sundry winds
As Fortune toileth in the affairs of kings,
That would be feared, yet fear to be beloved,   10
Sith fear or love to kings is flattery.
For instance, lordings, look upon your king,
By hate deprived of his dearest son,
The only hope of our successive line.

1 NOBLEMAN
I had not thought that Alexandro's heart   15
Had been envenomed with such extreme hate:
But now I see that words have several works,
And there's no credit in the countenance.

VILLUPPO
No, for, my lord, had you beheld the train
That feigned love had coloured in his looks,   20
When he in camp consorted Balthazar,
Far more inconstant had you thought the sun,
That hourly coasts the centre of the earth,
Than Alexandro's purpose to the prince.

VICEROY
No more, Villuppo, thou hast said enough,   25
And with thy words thou slay'st our wounded thoughts.
Nor shall I longer dally with the world,
Procrastinating Alexandro's death:
Go some of you and fetch the traitor forth,

10 *would be* wish to be
11 *Sith* since
12 *lordings* lords
14 *successive line* line of succession
15 s.p 1 NOBLEMAN ed. (*Nob. 1592*)
17 *words have several works* i.e. what a man does may not always reflect what he
   says
18 *no credit in* no point in trusting
19–20 'if you had seen the false appearance [of friendship] that pretended love had
   counterfeited in his face.' 'Train' literally means 'treachery'; Villuppo uses the
   word to describe the false appearance of love (a treacherous mask) Alexandro is
   accused of wearing.
21 *consorted* associated with, kept company with
23 *That hourly ... earth* 'that with a regular motion (in a precise number of hours)
   circles this earth, the centre of the universe.' Kyd writes in terms of the old
   cosmology; the sun's (apparent) circling often served as a metaphor for
   constancy.
24 *purpose* attitude, relationship

That as he is condemned he may die.   30

Enter ALEXANDRO *with a* NOBLEMAN *and* HALBERTS

2 NOBLEMAN
   In such extremes will naught but patience serve.
ALEXANDRO
   But in extremes what patience shall I use?
   Nor discontents it me to leave the world,
   With whom there nothing can prevail but wrong.
2 NOBLEMAN
   Yet hope the best.
ALEXANDRO   'Tis Heaven is my hope.   35
   As for the earth, it is too much infect
   To yield me hope of any of her mould.
VICEROY
   Why linger ye? bring forth that daring fiend,
   And let him die for his accursed deed.
ALEXANDRO
   Not that I fear the extremity of death,   40
   For nobles cannot stoop to servile fear,
   Do I, O king, thus discontented live.
   But this, O this, torments my labouring soul,
   That thus I die suspected of a sin,
   Whereof, as heavens have known my secret thoughts,   45
   So am I free from this suggestion.
VICEROY
   No more, I say! to the tortures! when!
   Bind him, and burn his body in those flames,
                 They bind him to the stake
   That shall prefigure those unquenched fires

30 s.d. HALBERTS halberdiers; see I, iv, 21 note.
31 s.p. 2 NOBLEMAN ed. (*Nob. 1592*)
32–7 Alexandro's sense of life's injustices anticipates much that Hieronimo has to
    say in the next scene: part of the 'overlapping' technique Kyd uses so
    successfully (see III, ii, 3 ff.).
34 *With . . . wrong* i.e. since all I ever meet is injustice
36 *infect* infected
37 *To yield . . . mould* i.e. to allow me to place any faith in anyone born and brought
    up there
46 *suggestion* false accusation (*O.E.D.*, 3)
47 *when!* an impatient exclamation
48 Hattaway (p. 122) remarks that the audience will have known that flames
    would not be lighted in the playhouse, thus anticipating Alexandro's release,
    and reading the incident in emblematic rather than realistic terms.

Of Phlegethon prepared for his soul.   50

ALEXANDRO

My guiltless death will be avenged on thee,
On thee, Villuppo, that hath maliced thus,
Or for thy meed hast falsely me accused.

VILLUPPO

Nay, Alexandro, if thou menace me,
I'll lend a hand to send thee to the lake   55
Where those thy words shall perish with thy works –
Injurious traitor, monstrous homicide!

Enter AMBASSADOR

AMBASSADOR

Stay, hold a while,
And here, with pardon of his majesty,
Lay hands upon Villuppo.

VICEROY   Ambassador,   60

What news hath urged this sudden entrance?

AMBASSADOR

Know, sovereign lord, that Balthazar doth live.

VICEROY

What say'st thou? liveth Balthazar our son?

AMBASSADOR

Your highness' son, Lord Balthazar, doth live;
And, well entreated in the court of Spain,   65
Humbly commends him to your majesty.
These eyes beheld, and these my followers;
With these, the letters of the king's commends,

Gives him letters

Are happy witnesses of his highness' health.

The VICEROY *looks on the letters, and proceeds*

VICEROY

[*Reads*] 'Thy son doth live, your tribute is received,   70
Thy peace is made, and we are satisfied.

---

50 *Phlegethon* the mythical river of hell whose waves were of fire
52 *maliced* entertained malice (*O.E.D.*, v, 2)
53 *meed* reward, advantage
55 *lake* the lake of Acheron in hell, into which Phlegethon (l. 50) flows
58–61 lineation ed. (Stay...Maiestie,/Lay...Villuppo./Embassadour... entrance?
     1592)
61 *entrance* three syllables   68 *commends* greetings
69 s.d. VICEROY ed. (*King 1592*)

The rest resolve upon as things proposed
For both our honours and thy benefit.'

AMBASSADOR

These are his highness' farther articles.

He gives him more letters

VICEROY

Accursed wretch, to intimate these ills   75
Against the life and reputation
Of noble Alexandro! Come, my lord,
Let him unbind thee that is bound to death,
To make a quital for thy discontent.

They unbind him

ALEXANDRO

Dread lord, in kindness you could do no less,   80
Upon report of such a damned fact.
But thus we see our innocence hath saved
The hopeless life which thou, Villuppo, sought
By thy suggestions to have massacred.

VICEROY

Say, false Villuppo, wherefore didst thou thus   85
Falsely betray Lord Alexandro's life?
Him, whom thou knowest that no unkindness else,
But even the slaughter of our dearest son,
Could once have moved us to have misconceived.

ALEXANDRO

Say, treacherous Villuppo, tell the king,   90
Wherein hath Alexandro used thee ill?

VILLUPPO

Rent with remembrance of so foul a deed,
My guilty soul submits me to thy doom:

72 *resolve upon* decide upon
75 *intimate* make known, announce publicly
77 *Come, my lord*, ed. *1592* adds 'vnbinde him', but this gives the line thirteen
   syllables. The extra words may have been included into the text from a stage-
   direction placed too early (and not cancelled when the direction at l. 79 was
   added), or they may result from a compositor's anticipation of that direction.
   Edwards must be right to omit them.
79 *quital* requital, recompense
79 s.d. Villuppo unbinds Alexandro as the text directs; 'they unbind him' is used to
   mean 'he is unbound'.
80 *in kindness* by your nature (as a king)
81 *fact* deed   82 *our* my
84 *suggestions* false accusations
89 *misconceived* suspected, formed a wrong opinion of
91 *Wherein* ed. (Or wherein *1592*)   93 *doom* judgment

For not for Alexandro's injuries,
But for reward and hope to be preferred,   95
Thus have I shamelessly hazarded his life.

VICEROY
Which, villain, shall be ransomed with thy death,
And not so mean a torment as we here
Devised for him who thou said'st slew our son,
But with the bitterest torments and extremes   100
That may be yet invented for thine end.

                          ALEXANDRO *seems to entreat*
Entreat me not, go, take the traitor hence.
                          Exit VILLUPPO [*guarded*]
And, Alexandro, let us honour thee
With public notice of thy loyalty.
To end those things articulated here   105
By our great lord, the mighty King of Spain,
We with our Council will deliberate.
Come, Alexandro, keep us company.   *Exeunt*

Act III, Scene ii

Enter HIERONIMO

HIERONIMO
O eyes, no eyes, but fountains fraught with tears;
O life, no life, but lively form of death;
O world, no world, but mass of public wrongs,
Confused and filled with murder and misdeeds!
O sacred heavens! if this unhallowed deed,   5
If this inhuman and barbarous attempt,

98 *mean* moderate
105 *articulated* contained in the proposals (or articles) sent by the King of Spain
    (see l. 74)
  1 ff. When Bobadil and Matthew discuss plays (in *Everyman in his Humour*, I,
    iv) they reserve their highest (clownish) praise for this speech; and thus convey
    Jonson's scorn for Kyd's 'conceited' oratorical style (Jonson may himself have
    acted Hieronimo). Sympathetic modern critics think otherwise: Clemen's
    analysis (pp. 271-5) shows the speech as 'a masterpiece of rhetorical art. Its
    structure and proportions are worked out with an almost mathematical
    exactness, and a variety of stylistic figures are harmoniously dovetailed in order
    to make a powerful emotional impact.'
  1 *fraught* filled
  2 *lively form of death* death with the appearance of life
  4 *Confused* disordered

If this incomparable murder thus
Of mine, but now no more my son,
Shall unrevealed and unrevengéd pass,
How should we term your dealings to be just,   10
If you unjustly deal with those that in your justice trust?
The night, sad secretary to my moans,
With direful visions wake my vexed soul,
And with the wounds of my distressful son
Solicit me for notice of his death.   15
The ugly fiends do sally forth of hell,
And frame my steps to unfrequented paths,
And fear my heart with fierce inflamed thoughts.
The cloudy day my discontents records,
Early begins to register my dreams   20
And drive me forth to seek the murderer.
Eyes, life, world, heavens, hell, night, and day,
See, search, show, send some man, some mean, that may –
                              A letter falleth

What's here? a letter? tush, it is not so!
A letter written to Hieronimo!   *Red ink*   25
[*Reads*] 'For want of ink, receive this bloody writ.
Me hath my hapless brother hid from thee:
Revenge thyself on Balthazar and him,
For these were they that murderéd thy son.
Hieronimo, revenge Horatio's death,   30
And better fare than Bel-imperia doth.'
What means this unexpected miracle?
My son slain by Lorenzo and the prince!
What cause had they Horatio to malign?
Or what might move thee, Bel-imperia,   35
To accuse thy brother, had he been the mean?

12 *secretary* confidant
13 *wake* plural for singular; Edwards compares solicit (l. 15) and drive (l. 21)
14 *distressful* causing distress, or distressed
18 *fear* frighten
23 *See ... may* – ed. (See ... some man,/Some ... may: *1592*)
23 *mean* means, way
23 s.d. The pat arrival of the letter may be intended to emphasise how accident,
    under the direction of Revenge, favours the ultimate working-out of vengeance.
25 s.d. *Red ink* probably an author's note that the letter should be seen to have been
    written in red
26 'For ed. (*Bel.* For *1592*)
26 *writ* writing, document
27 *hapless* luckless; perhaps 'attended with ill-luck'
32 *What* ed. (*Hiero* What *1592*)   34 *malign* hate

Hieronimo, beware, thou art betrayed,
And to entrap thy life this train is laid.
Advise thee therefore, be not credulous:
This is devised to endanger thee,   40
That thou by this Lorenzo shouldst accuse,
And he, for thy dishonour done, should draw
Thy life in question, and thy name in hate.
Dear was the life of my beloved son,
And of his death behoves me be revenged: 45
Then hazard not thine own, Hieronimo,
But live t'effect thy resolution.
I therefore will by circumstances try
What I can gather to confirm this writ,
And, hearkening near the Duke of Castile's house,   50
Close if I can with Bel-imperia,
To listen more, but nothing to bewray.

Enter PEDRINGANO

Now Pedringano!
PEDRINGANO   Now, Hieronimo!
HIERONIMO
Where's thy lady?
PEDRINGANO   I know not; here's my lord.

Enter LORENZO

LORENZO
How now, who's this? Hieronimo?
HIERONIMO   My lord.   55
PEDRINGANO
He asketh for my lady Bel-imperia.
LORENZO
What to do, Hieronimo? The duke my father hath
Upon some disgrace awhile removed her hence;
But if it be aught I may inform her of,
Tell me, Hieronimo, and I'll let her know it.   60
HIERONIMO
Nay, nay, my lord, I thank you, it shall not need.
I had a suit unto her, but too late,

38 *train* plot, trap
47 *t'effect thy resolution* to bring about what you have resolved
48 *by circumstances* by observing how they act; by gathering circumstantial
   evidence
51 *Close* meet; come to an understanding
52 *bewray* disclose

And her disgrace makes me unfortunate.

LORENZO
Why so, Hieronimo? use me.

HIERONIMO
O no, my lord, I dare not, it must not be,   65
I humbly thank your lordship.

LORENZO   Why then, farewell.

HIERONIMO
My grief no heart, my thoughts no tongue can tell.   *Exit*

LORENZO
Come hither, Pedringano, see'st thou this?

PEDRINGANO
My lord, I see it, and suspect it too.

LORENZO
This is that damned villain Serberine,   70
That hath, I fear, revealed Horatio's death.

PEDRINGANO
My lord, he could not, 'twas so lately done;
And since, he hath not left my company.

LORENZO
Admit he have not, his condition's such,
As fear or flattering words may make him false.   75
I know his humour, and therewith repent
That e'er I used him in this enterprise.
But Pedringano, to prevent the worst,
And 'cause I know thee secret as my soul,
Here, for thy further satisfaction, take thou this,   80
                Gives him more gold
And hearken to me. Thus it is devised:
This night thou must, and prithee so resolve,
Meet Serberine at Saint Luigi's Park –
Thou know'st 'tis here hard by behind the house.
There take thy stand, and see thou strike him sure,   85
For die he must, if we do mean to live.

PEDRINGANO
But how shall Serberine be there, my lord?

LORENZO
Let me alone, I'll send to him to meet
The prince and me, where thou must do this deed.

64 *use me* put your suit to me
74 *condition* nature, temperament
76 *humour* disposition
83 *Saint Luigi's* ed. (S. Liugis 1592)
88 *Let me alone* leave it to me

PEDRINGANO

   It shall be done, my lord, it shall be done,   90
   And I'll go arm myself to meet him there.

LORENZO

   When things shall alter, as I hope they will,
   Then shalt thou mount for this: thou know'st my mind.

                                 Exit PEDRINGANO

   Che le Ieron!

                    Enter PAGE

PAGE   My lord?

LORENZO   Go, sirrah, to Serberine,
   And bid him forthwith meet the prince and me   95
   At Saint Luigi's Park, behind the house,
   This evening, boy.

PAGE   I go, my lord.

LORENZO

   But, sirrah, let the hour be eight o'clock.
   Bid him not fail.

PAGE   I fly, my lord.   *Exit*

LORENZO

   Now to confirm the complot thou hast cast   100
   Of all these practices, I'll spread the watch,
   Upon precise commandment from the king,
   Strongly to guard the place where Pedringano
   This night shall murder hapless Serberine.
   Thus must we work that will avoid distrust,   105
   Thus must we practise to prevent mishap,

---

93 *mount* rise (socially); with a punning reference to 'mounting' the gallows, as he
    does; cf. II, iv, 60–1 on Horatio's similar rise
94 *Che le Ieron!* unexplained; perhaps, as Boas suggests, a corruption of the page's
    name. Freeman (p. 68) offers the suggestion that 'Che le' is equivalent to Italian
    'chi là' (Who [is] there?) and Ieron either the page's name or an abbreviation of
    Hieronimo; in the latter case the phrase would be prompted by Lorenzo's
    hearing a noise. This suggestion seems rather implausible dramatically.
94–7 lineation ed. (Goe . . . forthwith,/Meet . . . Parke,/Behinde . . . boy. *1592*)
96 *Saint Luigi's* ed. (*S. Liugis 1592*)
100 *complot* conspiracy
100 *cast* devised
101 *practices* deceits, plots
101 *spread the watch* position the constables
105–19 a speech full of sentiments typical of the Elizabethan 'Machiavellian'
105 *distrust* suspicion
106 *practise* scheme

And thus one ill another must expulse.
This sly enquiry of Hieronimo
For Bel-imperia breeds suspicion,
And this suspicion bodes a further ill.   110
As for myself, I know my secret fault;
And so do they, but I have dealt for them.
They that for coin their souls endangered,
To save my life, for coin shall venture theirs:
And better it's that base companions die,   115
Than by their life to hazard our good haps.
Nor shall they live, for me to fear their faith:
I'll trust myself, myself shall be my friend,
For die they shall, slaves are ordained to no other end.

Exit

Act III, Scene iii

Enter PEDRINGANO *with a pistol*

PEDRINGANO
Now, Pedringano, bid thy pistol hold;
And hold on, Fortune! once more favour me;
Give but success to mine attempting spirit,
And let me shift for taking of mine aim!
Here is the gold, this is the gold proposed: 5
It is no dream that I adventure for,
But Pedringano is possessed thereof.
And he that would not strain his conscience
For him that thus his liberal purse hath stretched,
Unworthy such a favour may he fail,   10
And, wishing, want, when such as I prevail.
As for the fear of apprehension,
I know, if need should be, my noble lord

107 *expulse* expel
108–9 lineation ed. (This ... suspition, *one line 1592*)
115 *it's* ed. (its *1592*)   115 *base companions* low-bred, vulgar fellows
116 *good haps* good fortune, security
117 *fear their faith* be apprehensive about their keeping faith
119 *slaves* mean, worthless fellows
  1 *hold* be true, function properly
  2 *hold on* continue, be consistent
  4 *let me shift* leave it to me
  7 *is possessed thereof* actually has the gold in his grasp
 10 *fail* be unsuccessful, fall into poverty

Will stand between me and ensuing harms;
Besides, this place is free from all suspect.   15
Here therefore will I stay and take my stand.

Enter the WATCH

1 WATCH
I wonder much to what intent it is
That we are thus expressly charged to watch.
2 WATCH
'Tis by commandment in the king's own name.
3 WATCH
But we were never wont to watch and ward   20
So near the duke his brother's house before.
2 WATCH
Content yourself, stand close, there's somewhat in't.

Enter SERBERINE

SERBERINE
Here, Serberine, attend and stay thy pace,
For here did Don Lorenzo's page appoint
That thou by his command shouldst meet with him.   25
How fit a place, if one were so disposed,
Methinks this corner is, to close with one.
PEDRINGANO
Here comes the bird that I must seize upon;
Now, Pedringano, or never, play the man!
SERBERINE
I wonder that his lordship stays so long,   30
Or wherefore should he send for me so late?
PEDRINGANO
For this, Serberine, and thou shalt ha't.

Shoots the dag
So, there he lies, my promise is performed.

The WATCH [*come forward*]

1 WATCH
Hark gentlemen, this is a pistol shot.

---

15 *suspect* suspicion
20 *watch and ward* patrol, keep guard; 'originally part of the legal definition of the
       duties of a sentinel' (Edwards)
22 *close* concealed
23 *stay thy pace* cease walking
27 *close with* grapple with, attack at close quarters (*O.E.D.*, v, 13)
32 s.d. *dag* a heavy pistol

2 WATCH
    And here's one slain; stay the murderer.   35
PEDRINGANO
    Now by the sorrows of the souls in hell,
                       He strives with the WATCH
    Who first lays hand on me, I'll be his priest.
3 WATCH
    Sirrah, confess, and therein play the priest;
    Why hast thou thus unkindly killed the man?
PEDRINGANO
    Why? because he walked abroad so late.   40
3 WATCH
    Come sir, you had been better kept your bed,
    Than have committed this misdeed so late.
2 WATCH
    Come, to the marshal's with the murderer!
1 WATCH
    On to Hieronimo's! help me here
    To bring the murdered body with us too.   45
PEDRINGANO
    Hieronimo? Carry me before whom you will,
    Whate'er he be I'll answer him and you.
    And do your worst, for I defy you all.   *Exeunt*

Act III, Scene iv

Enter LORENZO *and* BALTHAZAR

BALTHAZAR
    How now, my lord, what makes you rise so soon?
LORENZO
    Fear of preventing our mishaps too late.
BALTHAZAR
    What mischief is it that we not mistrust?

35 *stay* arrest
37 *I'll be his priest* i.e. I'll be there at his death; I'll make an end of him
39 *unkindly* inhumanly, against nature
40 *abroad* out of doors
43 *Come,* ed. (Come *1592*)
 2 *preventing* forestalling
 3 *mistrust* 'suspect the existence of or anticipate the occurrence of [something evil]' (*O.E.D.*, v, 3)

LORENZO

Our greatest ills we least mistrust, my lord,
And inexpected harms do hurt us most.   5

BALTHAZAR

Why tell me Don Lorenzo, tell me man,
If aught concerns our honour and your own.

LORENZO

Nor you nor me, my lord, but both in one;
For I suspect, and the presumption's great,
That by those base confederates in our fault   10
Touching the death of Don Horatio,
We are betrayed to old Hieronimo.

BALTHAZAR

Betrayed, Lorenzo? tush, it cannot be.

LORENZO

A guilty conscience, urged with the thought
Of former evils, easily cannot err: 15
I am persuaded, and dissuade me not,
That all's revealed to Hieronimo.
And therefore know that I have cast it thus –

[Enter PAGE]

But here's the page. How now, what news with thee?

PAGE

My lord, Serberine is slain.   20

BALTHAZAR

Who? Serberine, my man?

PAGE

Your highness' man, my lord.

LORENZO

Speak page, who murdered him?

PAGE

He that is apprehended for the fact.

LORENZO

Who?   25

PAGE

Pedringano.

BALTHAZAR

Is Serberine slain, that loved his lord so well?
Injurious villain, murderer of his friend!

---

5 *inexpected* ed. (in expected *1592*)
10 *confederates in our fault* partners in crime
18 *cast it thus* laid these plans
24 *fact* deed, crime

LORENZO

    Hath Pedringano murdered Serberine?

    My lord, let me entreat you to take the pains   30

    To exasperate and hasten his revenge

    With your complaints unto my lord the king.

    This their dissension breeds a greater doubt.

BALTHAZAR

    Assure thee, Don Lorenzo, he shall die,

    Or else his highness hardly shall deny.   35

    Meanwhile I'll haste the Marshal-Sessions,

    For die he shall for this his damned deed.

                             Exit BALTHAZAR

LORENZO

    Why so, this fits our former policy,

    And thus experience bids the wise to deal:

    I lay the plot, he prosecutes the point;   40

    I set the trap, he breaks the worthless twigs,

    And sees not that wherewith the bird was limed.

    Thus hopeful men, that mean to hold their own,

    Must look like fowlers to their dearest friends.

    He runs to kill whom I have holp to catch,   45

    And no man knows it was my reaching fatch.

    'Tis hard to trust unto a multitude,

    Or anyone, in mine opinion,

    When men themselves their secrets will reveal.

          Enter a MESSENGER *with a letter*

    Boy!   50

PAGE

    My lord?

LORENZO

    What's he?

MESSENGER   I have a letter to your lordship.

---

31 *exasperate* make harsher

32 *complaints* outcries, statements of grievance

33 *doubt* fear

35 *hardly shall deny* either 'refuse only with difficulty' or (as Edwards suggests) 'show harshness in denying me'

38-49 This is another typical speech of Machiavellian 'policy', where the main aim was to manipulate others.

40 *prosecutes the point* brings about the goal aimed at

42 *limed* caught in bird-lime

45 *holp* helped

46 *reaching* penetrating, designing

46 *fatch* stratagem (equals 'fetch', *O.E.D.*, sb. 1, 2)

LORENZO

From whence?

MESSENGER   From Pedringano that's imprisoned.

LORENZO

So he is in prison then?

MESSENGER   Ay, my good lord.

LORENZO

What would he with us? He writes us here   55
To stand good lord and help him in distress.
Tell him I have his letters, know his mind,
And what we may, let him assure him of.
Fellow, begone: my boy shall follow thee.

                                         Exit MESSENGER

This works like wax; yet once more try thy wits.   60
Boy, go convey this purse to Pedringano,
Thou knowest the prison, closely give it him,
And be advised that none be there about.
Bid him be merry still, but secret;
And though the Marshal-Sessions be today,   65
Bid him not doubt of his delivery.
Tell him his pardon is already signed,
And thereon bid him boldly be resolved;
For, were he ready to be turned off
(As 'tis my will the uttermost be tried)   70
Thou with his pardon shalt attend him still.
Show him this box, tell him his pardon's in't,
But open't not, and if thou lov'st thy life,
But let him wisely keep his hopes unknown;
He shall not want while Don Lorenzo lives.   75
Away!

PAGE   I go my lord, I run.

LORENZO

But sirrah, see that this be cleanly done.   *Exit* PAGE
Now stands our fortune on a tickle point,

55–6 lineation ed. (What ... vs?/He ... distres. *1592*)

56 *stand good lord* act as good lord and protector

60 *works like wax* follows my design (as wax is easily moulded and formed)

62 *closely* secretly

63 *be advised* take care

68 *boldly be resolved* feel completely assured

69 *turned off* hanged (the prisoner is 'turned off' the support he stands on and so hanged; see III, vi, 104 s.d.)

73 *and if* if

75–6 lineation ed. (*one line 1592*)   77 *cleanly* efficiently

78 *tickle* precarious, finely balanced

And now or never ends Lorenzo's doubts.
One only thing is uneffected yet,   80
And that's to see the executioner.
But to what end? I list not trust the air
With utterance of our pretence therein,
For fear the privy whispering of the wind
Convey our words amongst unfriendly ears,   85
That lie too open to advantages.
E quel che voglio io, nessun lo sa;
Intendo io: quel mi basterà.   *Exit*

Act III, Scene v

Enter BOY *with the box*

PAGE

My master hath forbidden me to look in this box, and by
my troth 'tis likely, if he had not warned me, I should not
have had so much idle time; for we men's-kind in our
minority are like women in their uncertainty: that they are
most forbidden, they will soonest attempt. So I now. By my   5
bare honesty, here's nothing but the bare empty box. Were
it not sin against secrecy, I would say it were a piece of
gentleman-like knavery. I must go to Pedringano, and tell
him his pardon is in this box; nay, I would have sworn it,
had I not seen the contrary. I cannot choose but smile to   10
think how the villain will flout the gallows, scorn the

---

79 *doubts* fears
82 *list not* have no wish to
83 *pretence* design, intention
86 *advantages* taking advantage, getting the upper hand
87-8 *E quel . . . basterà* ed. (*Et quel que voglio Ii nessun le sa,/Intendo io quel mi
   bassara. 1592*) 'And what I wish, no one knows; *I* understand, that suffices me.'
   1 s.d. *the box*] Ardolino, 'Hangman's Noose' (pp. 336–40), associates the box with
   the mythological Pandora's box in which only hope was left when all human
   qualities, good or ill, had escaped. Such a reading sharpens the ironies of these
   two scenes. Barbara Baines, however, finds the Silenus box of Plato's
   Symposium, later used by Erasmus as a symbol for the discrepancy between
   appearance and reality, a more convincing analogy.
   1 s.p. PAGE ed. (*not in 1592*)
   4 *minority* while still boys
   4 *uncertainty* fearfulness
   11 *flout* jest at

audience, and descant on the hangman, and all presuming
of his pardon from hence. Will't not be an odd jest, for me
to stand and grace every jest he makes, pointing my finger
at this box, as who would say, 'Mock on, here's thy   15
warrant.' Is't not a scurvy jest that a man should jest
himself to death? Alas, poor Pedringano, I am in a sort
sorry for thee, but if I should be hanged with thee, I cannot
weep.   *Exit*

Act III, Scene vi

Enter HIERONIMO *and the* DEPUTY

HIERONIMO

Thus must we toil in other men's extremes,
That know not how to remedy our own;
And do them justice, when unjustly we,
For all our wrongs, can compass no redress.
But shall I never live to see the day   5
That I may come, by justice of the heavens,
To know the cause that may my cares allay?
This toils my body, this consumeth age,
That only I to all men just must be,
And neither gods nor men be just to me.   10

DEPUTY

Worthy Hieronimo, your office asks
A care to punish such as do transgress.

HIERONIMO

So is't my duty to regard his death
Who when he lived deserved my dearest blood.
But come, for that we came for, let's begin,   15

12 *descant on* hold forth about
16 *scurvy* bitter, base
 1 s.d. DEPUTY 'the official title of the assistant to the Knight Marshal' (Edwards)
 1 ff. This speech, and that at III, vii, 10 ff., is crucial to an understanding of
   Hieronimo's outlook at this stage in the play. Both speeches show, against
   hostile critics, Hieronimo's deep concern for justice (and not merely
   vengeance), together with his frustration at Heaven's apparent deafness.
 1 *extremes* difficulties, hardships
 7 *know the cause* experience the circumstance
 8 *toils* burdens   8 *consumeth age* wears out my life
13 *regard* care about, concern myself with
14 *deserved* merited my spilling
15 ed. (But come, for that we came for lets begin, *1592*)

For here lies that which bids me to be gone.

Enter OFFICERS, BOY, *and* PEDRINGANO, *with a letter in his hand, bound*

DEPUTY
Bring forth the prisoner, for the court is set.
PEDRINGANO
Gramercy, boy, but it was time to come;
For I had written to my lord anew
A nearer matter that concerneth him,   20
For fear his lordship had forgotten me.
But sith he hath remembered me so well –
Come, come, come on, when shall we to this gear?
HIERONIMO
Stand forth, thou monster, murderer of men,
And here, for satisfaction of the world,   25
Confess thy folly and repent thy fault,
For there's thy place of execution.
PEDRINGANO
This is short work! Well, to your marshalship
First I confess, nor fear I death therefore,
I am the man, 'twas I slew Serberine.   30
But sir, then you think this shall be the place
Where we shall satisfy you for this gear?
DEPUTY
Ay, Pedringano.
PEDRINGANO   Now I think not so.
HIERONIMO
Peace, impudent, for thou shalt find it so:
For blood with blood shall, while I sit as judge,   35

16 *here* Hieronimo touches his head or heart. Or possibly (as Boas thinks) he refers to the bloody handkercher.
17–104 Ardolino ('Hangman's Noose', pp. 334–6) argues this scene is based on the familiar *Commedia dell'arte lazzo* (or trick) in which the trickster, condemned to hanging, pretends not to understand how to put his head in the noose, has the hangman demonstrate, and hangs him instead. Pedringano, whose name may derive from the *commedia* wily servant, Pedrolino, fails in a parallel trick here, though his death brings to light the very information Lorenzo was trying to conceal.
18 *Gramercy* an exclamation of relief
20 *nearer* of greater concern, more serious
23 *gear* business
25 *for satisfaction of* to convince, demonstrate to
29 *therefore* 'therefor' may be the correct reading
32 *gear* action, behaviour

Be satisfied, and the law discharged.
And though myself cannot receive the like,
Yet will I see that others have their right.
Despatch, the fault's approvéd and confessed,
And by our law he is condemned to die.   40

HANGMAN
Come on sir, are you ready?

PEDRINGANO
To do what, my fine officious knave?

HANGMAN
To go to this gear.

PEDRINGANO
O sir, you are too forward; thou wouldst fain furnish me
with a halter, to disfurnish me of my habit. So I should go   45
out of this gear, my raiment, into that gear, the rope. But,
hangman, now I spy your knavery, I'll not change without
boot, that's flat.

HANGMAN
Come sir.

PEDRINGANO
So then, I must up?   50

HANGMAN
No remedy.

PEDRINGANO
Yes, but there shall be for my coming down.

HANGMAN
Indeed, here's a remedy for that.

PEDRINGANO
How? be turned off?

HANGMAN
Ay, truly; come, are you ready? I pray, sir, despatch, the   55
day goes away.

39 *approvéd* proved, shown openly
43 *this gear* i.e. hanging
44 *forward* presumptuous
44–8 prose ed. (O sir . . . habit./So . . . rope./But . . . flat. *1592*)
45 *disfurnish me of my habit* Pedringano refers to the custom of giving the hangman
   his victim's clothes. See note to ll. 17–104 associating this scene with the trick
   played on the hangman in the *commedia dell'arte*.
45 *habit* clothes
47–8 *without boot* without compensation, without some amends (*O.E.D.*, sb. 19)
54 *turned off* be thrust off the support and so hang
55 *despatch* work quickly
55–6 as prose ed. (I . . . ready/I . . . away. *1592*)

PEDRINGANO

What, do you hang by the hour? If you do, I may chance to
break your old custom.

HANGMAN

Faith, you have reason, for I am like to break your young
neck.   60

PEDRINGANO

Dost thou mock me, hangman? Pray God I be not
preserved to break your knave's pate for this.

HANGMAN

Alas, sir, you are a foot too low to reach it, and I hope you
will never grow so high while I am in the office.

PEDRINGANO

Sirrah, dost see yonder boy with the box in his hand?   65

HANGMAN

What, he that points to it with his finger?

PEDRINGANO

Ay, that companion.

HANGMAN

I know him not, but what of him?

PEDRINGANO

Dost thou think to live till his old doublet will make thee a
new truss?   70

HANGMAN

Ay, and many a fair year after, to truss up many an
honester man than either thou or he.

PEDRINGANO

What hath he in his box, as thou think'st?

HANGMAN

Faith, I cannot tell, nor I care not greatly. Methinks you
should rather hearken to your soul's health.   75

PEDRINGANO

Why, sirrah hangman, I take it that that is good for the
body is likewise good for the soul; and it may be, in that box
is balm for both.

57 *by the hour* at set times

67 *companion* fellow

70 *truss* a close-fitting jacket (*O.E.D.*, sb. 3a). To 'truss up' (l. 71) is to hang.

74-5 as prose ed. (Faith . . . greatly./Me thinks . . . health. *1592*)

75 *hearken to* care for

76-8 Ardolino ('Hangman's Noose', p. 339) associates the moral emptiness of
     Pedringano's lines here with Porphyry's moral explanation of the Pandora
     myth, where man places his trust in the delusive hope supposedly contained in
     the box of wordly gifts.

HANGMAN
   Well, thou art even the merriest piece of man's flesh that
   e'er groaned at my office door.   80
PEDRINGANO
   Is your roguery become an 'office' with a knave's name?
HANGMAN
   Ay, and that shall all they witness that see you seal it with a
   thief's name.
PEDRINGANO
   I prithee, request this good company to pray with me.
HANGMAN
   Ay marry sir, this is a good motion; my masters, you see   85
   here's a good fellow.
PEDRINGANO
   Nay, nay, now I remember me, let them alone till some
   other time, for now I have no great need.
HIERONIMO
   I have not seen a wretch so impudent!
   O monstrous times, where murder's set so light;   90
   And where the soul that should be shrined in heaven,
   Solely delights in interdicted things,
   Still wandering in the thorny passages
   That intercepts itself of happiness.
   Murder, O bloody monster, God forbid   95
   A fault so foul should 'scape unpunished.
   Despatch and see this execution done –
   This makes me to remember thee, my son.
                        Exit HIERONIMO
PEDRINGANO
   Nay soft, no haste.
DEPUTY
   Why, wherefore stay you? Have you hope of life?   100
PEDRINGANO
   Why, ay.
HANGMAN
   As how?

---

81 *Is your . . . 'office'* Pedringano mocks the high-sounding 'office' used to describe
   the hangman's low-born ('knave's') occupation.
85 *motion* suggestion, idea
93 *Still* always, for ever
94 Edwards explains 'which prevent it (the soul) from attaining happiness.' A
   more natural construction would arise if 'That' were a misprint for 'And',
   making 'soul' the subject of 'intercepts'; there are, however, no grounds for
   emendation.
99 *soft* wait a moment

PEDRINGANO
   Why, rascal, by my pardon from the king.
HANGMAN
   Stand you on that? then you shall off with this.

                                        He turns him off

DEPUTY
   So, executioner. Convey him hence,   105
   But let his body be unburied:
   Let not the earth be choked or infect
   With that which heaven contemns, and men neglect.

                                        Exeunt

Act III, Scene vii

Enter HIERONIMO

HIERONIMO
   Where shall I run to breathe abroad my woes,
   My woes whose weight hath wearied the earth?
   Or mine exclaims, that have surcharged the air
   With ceaseless plaints for my deceased son?
   The blustering winds, conspiring with my words,   5
   At my lament have moved the leafless trees,
   Disrobed the meadows of their flowered green,
   Made mountains marsh with spring-tides of my tears,
   And broken through the brazen gates of hell.
   Yet still tormented is my tortured soul   10

---

104 *Stand you on that?* Do you depend on that? The hangman then refers to the
    literal sense of 'stand'.
104 s.d. The property which has already done duty as an arbour may have again
    been used here (stripped, perhaps, of its leaves and branches) to effect this
    second hanging. But see II, iv, 53 s.d. and note.
108 *heaven* ed. (heauens *1592*)
  1 s.p. HIERONIMO ed. (*not in 1592*)   1 *breathe abroad* give expression to
  1-9 Hieronimo's language, and the implied stage action, may seem exaggerated
    and over-theatrical to modern readers; the speech is, however, very nicely
    calculated for stage delivery and may be played with restraint, while the
    wording very effectively conveys Hieronimo's total preoccupation with his
    son's death.
  3 *exclaims* cries
10-18 Hieronimo's sense of thwarted right, and the apparent indifference of 'the
    brightest heavens', are main elements in our sympathy for his cause. His state of
    mind predicts, if briefly and unsubtly, the baffled and thwarted questioning of
    Hamlet.

With broken sighs and restless passions,
That winged mount, and hovering in the air,
Beat at the windows of the brightest heavens,
Soliciting for justice and revenge;
But they are placed in those empyreal heights,   15
Where, counter-mured with walls of diamond,
I find the place impregnable; and they
Resist my woes, and give my words no way.

Enter HANGMAN *with a letter*

HANGMAN
O lord sir, God bless you sir, the man sir,
Petergade sir, he that was so full of merry conceits –   20
HIERONIMO
Well, what of him?
HANGMAN
O lord sir, he went the wrong way, the fellow had a fair
commission to the contrary. Sir, here is his passport; I pray
you sir, we have done him wrong.
HIERONIMO
I warrant thee, give it me.   25
HANGMAN
You will stand between the gallows and me?
HIERONIMO
Ay, ay.
HANGMAN
I thank your Lord Worship.   *Exit* HANGMAN
HIERONIMO
And yet, though somewhat nearer me concerns,
I will, to ease the grief that I sustain,   30
Take truce with sorrow while I read on this.
'My lord, I writ as mine extremes required,
That you would labour my delivery;
If you neglect, my life is desperate,

11 *passions* sufferings, protesting cries
15 *empyreal* of the highest heaven; the dwelling-place of God
16 *counter-mured* having two walls, one within the other
20 *Petergade* the hangman's bungling attempt at 'Pedringano'
20 *conceits* jests
22-3 *fair commission* proper written authority
32 *writ* ed. (write *1592*). The past tense must be correct; Pedringano refers to his
    previous letter.
32 *extremes* extreme position, predicament
34 *desperate* despaired of, without hope

And in my death I shall reveal the troth.   35
You know, my lord, I slew him for your sake;
And as confederate with the prince and you,
Won by rewards and hopeful promises,
I holp to murder Don Horatio too.'
Holp he to murder mine Horatio?   40
And actors in th' accursed tragedy
Wast thou, Lorenzo, Balthazar and thou,
Of whom my son, my son deserved so well?
What have I heard, what have mine eyes beheld?
O sacred heavens, may it come to pass   45
That such a monstrous and detested deed,
So closely smothered, and so long concealed,
Shall thus by this be vengéd or revealed!
Now see I what I durst not then suspect,
That Bel-imperia's letter was not feigned.   50
Nor feigned she, though falsely they have wronged
Both her, myself, Horatio and themselves.
Now may I make compare, 'twixt hers and this,
Of every accident; I ne'er could find
Till now, and now I feelingly perceive,   55
They did what heaven unpunished would not leave.
O false Lorenzo, are these thy flattering looks?
Is this the honour that thou didst my son?
And Balthazar, bane to thy soul and me,
Was this the ransom he reserved thee for?   60

37 *as* ed. (was *1592*)
37 *as confederate* Edwards's correction ('as' for 'was') gives good sense and syntax;
   Joseph's retention of 'was' on the grounds that three separate statements are
   involved is possible but strained.
45 ff. Hieronimo accepts that coincidences indicate Heaven's wish to bring about
   justice; a weakened form of the mediaeval belief in Fortune as God's servant.
47 *closely smothered* kept a close secret
50-1 *was not feigned. Nor feigned she* 'He is relieved of two doubts [see III, ii,
   37-52], whether or not Bel-imperia really wrote the letter, and if so whether or
   not she was telling the truth' (McIlwraith).
53-6 'Now I can check on every happening, by using the two letters; I could never
   be sure till now – but now I see very vividly – that they committed this crime
   which Heaven must and will punish.' Edwards, I take it, is correct in keeping
   (and giving greater weight to) *1592*'s stop after 'accident'.
54 *accident;* ed. (accident, *1592*) happening, occurrence (relating to Horatio's
   death)
54 *find* understand
55 *feelingly* vividly, with feeling
59 *bane* poison, cause of ruin

Woe to the cause of these constrained wars,
Woe to thy baseness and captivity,
Woe to thy birth, thy body and thy soul,
Thy cursed father, and thy conquered self!
And banned with bitter execrations be   65
The day and place where he did pity thee!
But wherefore waste I mine unfruitful words,
When naught but blood will satisfy my woes?
I will go plain me to my lord the king,
And cry aloud for justice through the court,   70
Wearing the flints with these my withered feet,
And either purchase justice by entreats
Or tire them all with my revenging threats.   *Exit*

Act III, Scene viii

Enter ISABELLA *and her* MAID

ISABELLA
So that, you say, this herb will purge the eye,
And this the head?
Ah, but none of them will purge the heart:
No, there's no medicine left for my disease,
Nor any physic to recure the dead.   5
                                      She runs lunatic
Horatio! O, where's Horatio?
MAID
Good madam, affright not thus yourself
With outrage for your son Horatio:
He sleeps in quiet in the Elysian fields.
ISABELLA
Why, did I not give you gowns and goodly things,   10
Bought you a whistle and a whipstalk too,

61 *constrained* forced, unnecessary   65 *banned* cursed
69 *plain* complain, plead
69–73 Hieronimo's impulse is to seek justice through the approved channels; only
    if he is thwarted will he take matters into his own hands.
  1–5 These lines may conceivably have suggested Ophelia's flower-lore in
    madness. Isabella will probably be dressed in this scene in the tattered garments
    and unbound hair conventionally associated with madness.
  1 *purge* cleanse, heal   2–3 lineation ed. (*one line 1592*)
  5 *recure* recover, restore to health   8 *outrage* outrageous behaviour, passion
  9 *Elysian fields* the place of the blessed in the afterworld
 11 *whipstalk* whip-handle; used, presumably, in a child's game

To be revenged on their villainies?
MAID
Madam, these humours do torment my soul.
ISABELLA
My soul! poor soul, thou talks of things
Thou know'st not what – my soul hath silver wings, 15
That mounts me up unto the highest heavens;
To heaven, ay, there sits my Horatio,
Backed with a troop of fiery cherubins,
Dancing about his newly-healed wounds,
Singing sweet hymns and chanting heavenly notes, 20
Rare harmony to greet his innocence,
That died, ay died a mirror in our days.
But say, where shall I find the men, the murderers,
That slew Horatio? Whither shall I run
To find them out that murdered my son? *Exeunt* 25

Act III, Scene ix

BEL-IMPERIA *at a window*

BEL-IMPERIA
What means this outrage that is offered me?
Why am I thus sequestered from the court?
No notice? Shall I not know the cause
Of this my secret and suspicious ills?
Accursed brother, unkind murderer, 5
Why bends thou thus thy mind to martyr me?
Hieronimo, why writ I of thy wrongs,
Or why art thou so slack in thy revenge?
Andrea, O Andrea, that thou sawest

---

13 *humours* uncontrolled fancies
14–22 Isabella's language here, perhaps only to secure pathos, is distinctly
   Christian in its description of the after-life, in contrast to the Virgilian language
   of most other references. Edwards has shown that Kyd's writing here may be
   indebted to Thomas Watson's elegy on Walsingham, published in 1590.
21 *greet* honour (*not*, as the context shows, 'welcome'); Edwards compares
   (*O.E.D.*, 3e) Spenser's use of the word to mean 'to offer congratulations'.
22 *mirror* model of excellence
 2 *sequestered* kept apart, secluded
 3 *No notice* kept in ignorance
 4 *suspicious* arousing suspicion
 5 *unkind* unnatural
 6 *bends* applies

Me for thy friend Horatio handled thus,   10
And him for me thus causeless murdered.
Well, force perforce, I must constrain myself
To patience, and apply me to the time,
Till heaven, as I have hoped shall set me free.

Enter CHRISTOPHIL

CHRISTOPHIL
Come, Madam Bel-imperia, this may not be.   *Exeunt*   15

Act III, Scene x

Enter LORENZO, BALTHAZAR, *and the* PAGE

LORENZO
Boy, talk no further, thus far things go well.
Thou art assured that thou sawest him dead?
PAGE
Or else my lord I live not.
LORENZO   That's enough.
As for his resolution in his end,
Leave that to him with whom he sojourns now.   5
Here, take my ring and give it Christophil,
And bid him let my sister be enlarged,
And bring her hither straight.   *Exit* PAGE
This that I did was for a policy
To smooth and keep the murder secret,   10
Which as a nine-days' wonder being o'erblown,
My gentle sister will I now enlarge.
BALTHAZAR
And time, Lorenzo, for my lord the duke,
You heard, enquired for her yester-night.
LORENZO
Why, and, my lord, I hope you heard me say   15
Sufficient reason why she kept away.
But that's all one. My lord, you love her?
BALTHAZAR   Ay.

---

12 *force perforce* of necessity

---

13 *apply me to the time* accept things as they are
 4 *resolution* courage
 7 *enlarged* set free
 9 *policy* stratagem, cunning purpose
10 *smooth* avoid difficult consequences

LORENZO

    Then in your love beware, deal cunningly,
    Salve all suspicions; only soothe me up;
    And if she hap to stand on terms with us,   20
    As for her sweetheart, and concealment so,
    Jest with her gently: under feigned jest
    Are things concealed that else would breed unrest.
    But here she comes.

Enter BEL-IMPERIA

                    Now, sister –

BEL-IMPERIA   Sister? No!

    Thou art no brother, but an enemy,   25
    Else wouldst thou not have used thy sister so:
    First, to affright me with thy weapons drawn,
    And with extremes abuse my company;
    And then to hurry me, like whirlwind's rage,
    Amidst a crew of thy confederates,   30
    And clap me up where none might come at me,
    Nor I at any, to reveal my wrongs.
    What madding fury did possess thy wits?
    Or wherein is't that I offended thee?

LORENZO

    Advise you better, Bel-imperia,   35
    For I have done you no disparagement;
    Unless, by more discretion than deserved,
    I sought to save your honour and mine own.

BEL-IMPERIA

    Mine honour! why, Lorenzo, wherein is't
    That I neglect my reputation so,   40
    As you, or any, need to rescue it?

LORENZO

    His highness and my father were resolved
    To come confer with old Hieronimo,

19 *Salve* allay
19 *soothe me up* agree with me
20 *stand on terms* argue, prove difficult
24 *Now* ed. (*Lor.* Now *1592*)
24–5 lineation ed. (But . . . comes./Now Sister./Sister . . . enemy. *1592*)
28 *extremes* harsh behaviour
31 *clap me up* lock me up unceremoniously
36 *disparagement* dishonour, humiliation
37 'unless it were that, showing more concern and foresight than you deserved . . . '

Concerning certain matters of estate,
That by the viceroy was determined.   45
BEL-IMPERIA
And wherein was mine honour touched in that?
BALTHAZAR
Have patience, Bel-imperia; hear the rest.
LORENZO
Me next in sight as messenger they sent,
To give him notice that they were so nigh:
Now when I came, consorted with the prince,   50
And unexpected, in an arbour there,
Found Bel-imperia with Horatio –
BEL-IMPERIA
How then?
LORENZO
Why then, remembering that old disgrace,
Which you for Don Andrea had endured,   55
And now were likely longer to sustain,
By being found so meanly accompanied,
Thought rather, for I knew no readier mean,
To thrust Horatio forth my father's way.
BALTHAZAR
And carry you obscurely somewhere else,   60
Lest that his highness should have found you there.
BEL-IMPERIA
Even so, my lord? And you are witness
That this is true which he entreateth of?
You, gentle brother, forged this for my sake,
And you, my lord, were made his instrument: 65
A work of worth, worthy the noting too!
But what's the cause that you concealed me since?
LORENZO
Your melancholy, sister, since the news
Of your first favourite Don Andrea's death,

44–5 Edwards, citing *O.E.D.*, explains: 'concerning certain matters about posses-
    sions which the viceroy had given up.' 'Determined' might, however, mean more
    simply 'decided' or 'specified', and 'matters of estate' might mean 'matters of
    importance', 'state-matters'.
48 *next in sight* standing nearby
54 *that old disgrace* See I, 1, 10–11 and note.
57 *meanly* by a man of low rank. Horatio's inferior social standing is frequently
    emphasised.
64 *forged* devised and executed this course of action; with an ironic hint of the
    modern sense of deceit

My father's old wrath hath exasperate.   70

BALTHAZAR

And better was't for you, being in disgrace,
To absent yourself, and give his fury place.

BEL-IMPERIA

But why had I no notice of his ire?

LORENZO

That were to add more fuel to your fire,
Who burnt like Aetna for Andrea's loss.   75

BEL-IMPERIA

Hath not my father then enquired for me?

LORENZO

Sister, he hath, and thus excused I thee.

                He whispereth in her ear

But, Bel-imperia, see the gentle prince;
Look on thy love, behold young Balthazar,
Whose passions by thy presence are increased;   80
And in whose melancholy thou may'st see
Thy hate, his love; thy flight, his following thee.

BEL-IMPERIA

Brother, you are become an orator –
I know not, I, by what experience –
Too politic for me, past all compare,   85
Since last I saw you; but content yourself,
The prince is meditating higher things.

BALTHAZAR

'Tis of thy beauty, then, that conquers kings;
Of those thy tresses, Ariadne's twines,
Wherewith my liberty thou hast surprised;   90

---

70 *exasperate* made harsher

72 *give his fury place* allow his wrath to expend itself harmlessly

75 *Aetna* the volcano in Sicily

77 s.d. Where others have thought this clumsy, Kay (p. 29) regards it as a
deliberate device, part of Kyd's systematic and unsettling denial of information
to the theatre-audience.

85 *Too politic* This refers to the 'orator' (who has become too cunning), and not to
'experience'.

89 *Ariadne's* Kyd probably has in mind here Arachne, the Lydian weaver whom
Athene changed to a spider; Ariadne, daughter of King Minos of Crete, did,
however, use a thread in guiding Theseus through the labyrinth. Neither is
especially apt here.

89 *twines* threads, cords

90 *surprised* captured

Of that thine ivory front, my sorrow's map,
Wherein I see no haven to rest my hope.
BEL-IMPERIA
To love and fear, and both at once, my lord,
In my conceit, are things of more import
Than women's wits are to be busied with.   95
BALTHAZAR
'Tis I that love.
BEL-IMPERIA   Whom?
BALTHAZAR   Bel-imperia.
BEL-IMPERIA
But I that fear.
BALTHAZAR   Whom?
BEL-IMPERIA   Bel-imperia.
LORENZO
Fear yourself?
BEL-IMPERIA   Ay, brother.
LORENZO   How?
BEL-IMPERIA   As those
That what they love are loath and fear to lose.
BALTHAZAR
Then, fair, let Balthazar your keeper be.   100
BEL-IMPERIA
No, Balthazar doth fear as well as we:
Et tremulo metui pavidum junxere timorem,
Et vanum stolidae proditionis opus.   *Exit*
LORENZO
Nay and you argue things so cunningly,
We'll go continue this discourse at court.   105
BALTHAZAR
Led by the loadstar of her heavenly looks,
Wends poor oppressed Balthazar,
As o'er the mountains walks the wanderer,
Incertain to effect his pilgrimage.   *Exeunt*

---

91 *front* forehead
91 *sorrow's map* The forehead was supposed to reflect feelings; it is a 'map' because
   Balthazar seeks its aid in discovering the success of his proposal.
94 *In my conceit* to my mind, in my judgment
98–9 lineation ed. (*one line 1592*)
102 *Et* ed. (*Est 1592*)
102–3 'They yoked craven fear to trembling dread: and that a fruitless work of
   doltish treason.' It is difficult to make of these lines a more than very general
   sense.
106 *loadstar* a star to steer by, usually in reference to the pole-star
109 *Incertain to effect* with no confidence of being able to complete

Act III, Scene xi

Enter two PORTINGALES, *and* HIERONIMO *meets them*

1 PORTINGALE
  By your leave, sir.
HIERONIMO
  Good leave have you: nay, I pray you go,
  For I'll leave you; if you can leave me, so.
2 PORTINGALE
  Pray you, which is the next way to my lord the duke's?
HIERONIMO
  The next way from me.
1 PORTINGALE   To his house, we mean.   5
HIERONIMO
  O, hard by, 'tis yon house that you see.
2 PORTINGALE
  You could not tell us if his son were there?
HIERONIMO
  Who, my lord Lorenzo?
1 PORTINGALE   Ay, sir.
          He goeth in at one door and comes out at another
HIERONIMO   O, forbear,
  For other talk for us far fitter were.
  But if you be importunate to know   10
  The way to him, and where to find him out,
  Then list to me, and I'll resolve your doubt.
  There is a path upon your left-hand side,
  That leadeth from a guilty conscience
  Unto a forest of distrust and fear,   15
  A darksome place, and dangerous to pass:
  There shall you meet with melancholy thoughts,

1–8 Hieronimo's inconsequential talk, like Hamlet's 'wild and whirling words', is
  meant to convey the tension he is suffering under. The 'Third Addition',
  inserted after 1. 1, much expands this state of mind.
3 *me, so* ed. (me so *1592*)
4 *next* nearest
8–9 lineation ed. (*one line 1592*)
10 *be importunate* insist
13 Compare I, i, 63–71 and note. Lorenzo is, according to Hieronimo, in 'the
  deepest hell'.

Whose baleful humours if you but uphold,
It will conduct you to despair and death;
Whose rocky cliffs when you have once beheld,   20
Within a hugy dale of lasting night,
That, kindled with the world's iniquities,
Doth cast up filthy and detested fumes,
Not far from thence, where murderers have built
A habitation for their cursed souls,   25
There, in a brazen cauldron, fixed by Jove
In his fell wrath upon a sulphur flame,
Yourselves shall find Lorenzo bathing him
In boiling lead and blood of innocents.

1 PORTINGALE
Ha, ha, ha!
HIERONIMO   Ha, ha, ha!   30
Why, ha, ha, ha! Farewell, good, ha, ha, ha!   *Exit*
2 PORTINGALE
Doubtless this man is passing lunatic,
Or imperfection of his age doth make him dote.
Come, let's away to seek my lord the duke.

[*Exeunt*]

Act III, Scene xii

Enter HIERONIMO, *with a poniard in one hand, and a rope in
the other*

HIERONIMO
Now sir, perhaps I come and see the king,
The king sees me, and fain would hear my suit:
Why, is not this a strange and seld-seen thing,
That standers-by with toys should strike me mute?

18 *baleful humours* evil tendencies, habits of mind
18 *uphold* persist in
21 *hugy* huge, profound
22 *kindled* set on fire
27 *fell* cruel
30–1 lineation ed. (*one line 1592*)
32 *passing* exceedingly
33 *imperfection of his age* decrepitude, the declining powers of old age
 1 s.d. *poniard* dagger. Hieronimo carries, as Boas remarks, 'the stock "properties"
   of a would-be suicide' in Elizabethan drama.
 3 *seld* seldom
 4 *toys* trifles; trivial business

Go to, I see their shifts, and say no more.   5
Hieronimo, 'tis time for thee to trudge:
Down by the dale that flows with purple gore
Standeth a fiery tower; there sits a judge
Upon a seat of steel and molten brass,
And 'twixt his teeth he holds a fire-brand,   10
That leads unto the lake where hell doth stand.
Away, Hieronimo, to him be gone:
He'll do thee justice for Horatio's death.
Turn down this path, thou shalt be with him straight;
Or this, and then thou need'st not take thy breath.   15
This way or that way? Soft and fair, not so:
For if I hang or kill myself, let's know
Who will revenge Horatio's murder then?
No, no! fie, no! pardon me, I'll none of that:
                He flings away the dagger and halter
This way I'll take, and this way comes the king;   20
                He takes them up again
And here I'll have a fling at him, that's flat;
And, Balthazar, I'll be with thee to bring,
And thee, Lorenzo! Here's the king; nay, stay,
And here, ay here; there goes the hare away.

        Enter KING, AMBASSADOR, CASTILE, *and* LORENZO

KING
    Now show, Ambassador, what our viceroy saith: 25

5   *shifts* tricks
6   *trudge* get moving (*not* slowly)
7   *purple* blood-red
7 ff. Hieronimo's search for justice takes place in a landscape that directly recalls
    Andrea's search for a resting-place in the afterworld (see I, i); Kyd is anxious to
    draw out the analogies between the two quests.
11 *leads* shows the way to
14-15 *this path ... Or this* by killing himself with poniard or rope. Schick points
    out that ll. 14-19 present the same ideas as the last three lines of the Latin dirge
    (II, v, 78-80).
14 *straight* right away
17 *kill* stab
21 *that's flat* I have made up my mind
22 *I'll ... bring* I'll get even with you
24 *there ... away* Edwards explains the phrase refers to losing something one has
    tried to achieve or hold: Hieronimo sees the king passing by, preoccupied by
    business.
25-30 Hieronimo is thwarted by the day-to-day preoccupations of court business;
    as he foresaw at ll. 1-5.

Hath he received the articles we sent?

HIERONIMO

Justice, O, justice to Hieronimo.

LORENZO

Back, see'st thou not the king is busy?

HIERONIMO

O, is he so?

KING

Who is he that interrupts our business?   30

HIERONIMO

Not I. Hieronimo, beware: go by, go by.

AMBASSADOR

Renowned king, he hath received and read
Thy kingly proffers, and thy promised league,
And, as a man extremely overjoyed
To hear his son so princely entertained,   35
Whose death he had so solemnly bewailed,
This for thy further satisfaction
And kingly love, he kindly lets thee know:
First, for the marriage of his princely son
With Bel-imperia, thy beloved niece,   40
The news are more delightful to his soul,
Than myrrh or incense to the offended heavens.
In person, therefore, will he come himself,
To see the marriage rites solemnised;
And, in the presence of the court of Spain,   45
To knit a sure, inexplicable band
Of kingly love, and everlasting league,
Betwixt the crowns of Spain and Portingale,
There will he give his crown to Balthazar,
And make a queen of Bel-imperia.   50

KING

Brother, how like you this our viceroy's love?

CASTILE

No doubt, my lord, it is an argument
Of honourable care to keep his friend,
And wondrous zeal to Balthazar his son;

31 *go by, go by* beware, don't get into trouble
46 *inexplicable* ed. (inexecrable *1592*) which cannot be untied. *1594*'s reading,
   unique in that text for the extent of its departure from the earlier edition, is here
   preferred to *1592*'s 'inexecrable', on grounds of meaning. Edwards points out
   that *1594* might have been set up from a copy of *1592* which contained a
   corrected forme of inner G (and this reading); the sole surviving copy of *1592*
   would on that supposition contain an *uncorrected* inner G.
52 *argument* demonstration, proof

Nor am I least indebted to his grace,   55
That bends his liking to my daughter thus.

AMBASSADOR

Now last, dread lord, here hath his highness sent
(Although he send not that his son return)
His ransom due to Don Horatio.

HIERONIMO

Horatio! who calls Horatio?   60

KING

And well remembered, thank his majesty.
Here, see it given to Horatio.

HIERONIMO

Justice, O justice, justice, gentle king!

KING

What is that? Hieronimo?

HIERONIMO

Justice, O, justice! O my son, my son,   65
My son, whom naught can ransom or redeem!

LORENZO

Hieronimo, you are not well-advised.

HIERONIMO

Away, Lorenzo, hinder me no more,
For thou hast made me bankrupt of my bliss.
Give me my son, you shall not ransom him!   70
Away! I'll rip the bowels of the earth,
                              He diggeth with his dagger
And ferry over to th' Elysian plains,
And bring my son to show his deadly wounds.
Stand from about me!
I'll make a pickaxe of my poniard,   75
And here surrender up my marshalship:
For I'll go marshal up the fiends in hell,
To be avenged on you all for this.

KING

What means this outrage?
Will none of you restrain his fury?   80

56 *bends* directs
58 *that* in order that
62 The King alone seems unaware that Horatio is dead; an extremely implausible
   situation.
70 *you ... him* i.e., from death
72 *th'Elysian plains* See III, viii, 9 and note·.
74–5 lineation ed. (*one line 1592*)
79 *outrage* violent outburst
79–80 lineation ed. (*one line 1592*)

HIERONIMO

Nay, soft and fair: you shall not need to strive,
Needs must he go that the devils drive.   *Exit*

KING

What accident hath happed Hieronimo?
I have not seen him to demean him so.

LORENZO

My gracious lord, he is with extreme pride,   85
Conceived of young Horatio his son,
And covetous of having to himself
The ransom of the young prince Balthazar,
Distract, and in a manner lunatic.

KING

Believe me, nephew, we are sorry for't: 90
This is the love that fathers bear their sons.
But, gentle brother, go give to him this gold,
The prince's ransom; let him have his due.
For what he hath Horatio shall not want:
Haply Hieronimo hath need thereof.   95

LORENZO

But if he be thus helplessly distract,
'Tis requisite his office be resigned,
And given to one of more discretion.

KING

We shall increase his melancholy so.
'Tis best that we see further in it first;   100
Till when, ourself will exempt the place.
And brother, now bring in the ambassador,
That he may be a witness of the match
'Twixt Balthazar and Bel-imperia,
And that we may prefix a certain time,   105
Wherein the marriage shall be solemnised,
That we may have thy lord the viceroy here.

---

83 *happed* happened to   84 *demean him* behave himself
95 *Haply* perhaps
100 *see further in it* examine the business further
101 *ourself will exempt the place* I have retained the *1592* reading despite difficulties over the meaning of 'exempt' and despite the line's being one syllable short. The latter difficulty may not be a real one: the line would *act* perfectly well as it stands. 'Exempt' I take to mean something like 'hold in suspense': the King will avoid the indignity, for Hieronimo, of replacing him (Lorenzo's suggestion at ll. 96–8), and instead will continue the crown's judicial functions without an active Knight Marshal. Collier's emendation, 'execute', is attractive in that it presents the same idea more explicitly.
102 *bring in* escort to an inner room

AMBASSADOR
  Therein your highness highly shall content
  His majesty, that longs to hear from hence.
KING
  On, then, and hear you, Lord Ambassador.   *Exeunt*   110

Act III, Scene xiii

Enter HIERONIMO *with a book in his hand*

HIERONIMO
  Vindicta mihi!
  Ay, heaven will be revenged of every ill,
  Nor will they suffer murder unrepaid:
  Then stay, Hieronimo, attend their will,
  For mortal men may not appoint their time.   5
  'Per scelus semper tutum est sceleribus iter.'
  Strike, and strike home, where wrong is offered thee;
  For evils unto ills conductors be,
  And death's the worst of resolution.
  For he that thinks with patience to contend   10
  To quiet life, his life shall easily end.
  'Fata si miseros juvant, habes salutem;
  Fata si vitam negant, habes sepulchrum.'
  If destiny thy miseries do ease,
  Then hast thou health, and happy shalt thou be;   15

1 s.d. Hieronimo carries a copy of Seneca, as later quotations show.

1 s.p. HIERONIMO ed. (*not in 1592*)

1 *Vindicta mihi* Hieronimo quotes the Biblical admonition 'vengeance is mine; I will repay, saith the Lord' (Romans xii. 19), a statement much used by Elizabethan writers to reserve the execution of vengeance to God. The next four lines expand this attitude.

4 *attend their will* await Heaven's pleasure

6 'The safe way for crimes is through (further) crimes.' Hieronimo reads from the Seneca he holds in his hand (the Latin is an adaptation of Seneca's *Agamemnon*, l. 115). Prompted by the Senecan tag, he reflects that Lorenzo will probably try to secure his own safety by adding a crime against himself to the crime against Horatio (see ll. 10–11). It is this reflection that prompts his abandoning the argument for Christian patience of the first five lines.

9 *death's . . . resolution* death is the worst that can follow bold conduct

10 *contend* strive, make one's way

12–13 Again Hieronimo reads from Seneca (here *Troades*, ll. 511–12). The next four lines give a loose translation.

If destiny deny thee life, Hieronimo,
Yet shalt thou be assured of a tomb;
If neither, yet let this thy comfort be,
Heaven covereth him that hath no burial.
And to conclude, I will revenge his death!   20
But how? not as the vulgar wits of men,
With open, but inevitable ills,
As by a secret, yet a certain mean,
Which under kindship will be cloaked best.
Wise men will take their opportunity,   25
Closely and safely fitting things to time.
But in extremes advantage hath no time;
And therefore all times fit not for revenge.
Thus therefore will I rest me in unrest,
Dissembling quiet in unquietness,   30
Not seeming that I know their villainies;
That my simplicity may make them think
That ignorantly I will let all slip –
For ignorance, I wot, and well they know,
Remedium malorum iners est.   35

18 *neither* Presumably Hieronimo means neither health nor tomb.

21 *vulgar* common

22-3 rather clumsily expressed. Hieronimo means perhaps that simple-minded men ('vulgar wits') seek vengeance by methods which are bold and obvious ('open'), yet despite this effective; he, however, will use subtlety, though the subtlety will not endanger his plan's effectiveness. The main contrast is between crude force and the witty devices Hieronimo is considering.

22 *inevitable* inevitably successful

22 *ills* ill practices

23 *mean* course of action

24 *kindship* kindness

24 *cloaked* hidden

26 *Closely* with subtlety

26 *time* opportunity

27-8 'But' here means 'only'; Hieronimo says that only crises ('extremes') exclude the possibility of waiting for a favourable moment ('advantage'); revenge, being considered and deliberate, requires that one waits one's opportunity. Broude (pp. 138-9) explains that the recognition of opportunity (l. 25), the appropriate time for action, was a significant quality of the righteous man in Renaissance doctrine.

29-33 Hieronimo's proposed stealth need not conflict with his sense that Heaven prompts and supports him (see e.g. IV, i, 32-4 and III, vii, 45-56). Johnson (p. 29) quotes Calvin's remark that in dealing with the wicked 'God shewed himself a revenger by little and little, and as it were faire and softly' (i.e. stealthily).

32 *simplicity* apparently undesigning behaviour

35 'is an unskilful antidote to evils.' A further quotation from Seneca (adapted from *Oedipus* l. 515) but not, I think, read from the book.

Nor aught avails it me to menace them,
Who, as a wintry storm upon a plain,
Will bear me down with their nobility.
No, no, Hieronimo, thou must enjoin
Thine eyes to observation, and thy tongue   40
To milder speeches than thy spirit affords,
Thy heart to patience, and thy hands to rest,
Thy cap to courtesy, and thy knee to bow,
Till to revenge thou know, when, where and how.
                                        A noise within
How now, what noise? what coil is that you keep?   45

Enter a SERVANT

SERVANT
    Here are a sort of poor petitioners,
    That are importunate, and it shall please you, sir,
    That you should plead their cases to the king.
HIERONIMO
    That I should plead their several actions?
    Why, let them enter, and let me see them.   50

Enter three CITIZENS *and an* OLD MAN

1 CITIZEN
    So, I tell you this, for learning and for law,
    There's not any advocate in Spain
    That can prevail, or will take half the pain
    That he will, in pursuit of equity.
HIERONIMO
    Come near, you men, that thus importune me.   55
    [*Aside*] Now must I bear a face of gravity,
    For thus I used, before my marshalship,
    To plead in causes as corregidor. –
    Come on sirs, what's the matter?
2 CITIZEN   Sir, an action.

38 *nobility* noble rank
44 s.d. *follows l.45 in 1592*
45 *what coil ... keep?* what is all that noise you are making?
46 *sort* group, company
47 *and* if
49 *actions* cases in law
58 *corregidor* advocate. Strictly, Edwards notes, the chief magistrate of a Spanish
    town.

HIERONIMO
    Of battery?
1 CITIZEN   Mine of debt.
HIERONIMO   Give place.   60
2 CITIZEN
    No sir, mine is an action of the case.
3 CITIZEN
    Mine an *ejectione firmae* by a lease.
HIERONIMO
    Content you sirs, are you determined
    That I should plead your several actions?
1 CITIZEN
    Ay sir, and here's my declaration.   65
2 CITIZEN
    And here is my band.
3 CITIZEN   And here is my lease.
                    They give him papers

HIERONIMO
    But wherefore stands yon silly man so mute,
    With mournful eyes and hands to heaven upreared?
    Come hither, father, let me know thy cause.
SENEX
    O worthy sir, my cause, but slightly known,   70
    May move the hearts of warlike Myrmidons
    And melt the Corsic rocks with ruthful tears.
HIERONIMO
    Say, father, tell me what's thy suit?
SENEX
    No sir, could my woes
    Give way unto my most distressful words,   75
    Then should I not in paper, as you see,

---

61 *action of the case* An action not within the limited jurisdiction of the Common
   Pleas needed a special writ to cover it. These special writs were known as
   'actions of trespass on the case' or 'actions on the case' (Edwards).
62 *ejectione firmae* 'a writ to eject a tenant from his holding before the expiration of
   his lease' (Edwards). Kyd's 'by a lease' is difficult to account for.
62 *firmae* ed. (firma *1592*)
65 *declaration* in law, the plaintiff's statement of claim
66 *band* bond; the special writ referred to at l. 61 and note
67 *silly* simple, pitiable
71 *Myrmidons* Achilles' followers; a Thessalian tribe noted for their fierceness
72 *Corsic* of Corsica; Seneca's *Octavia* (II.i. in Newton's ed., 1581) has a reference
   to the 'craggy corsicke rockes' among which Seneca lived in exile.

With ink bewray what blood began in me.

HIERONIMO

What's here? 'The humble supplication
Of Don Bazulto for his murdered son.'

SENEX

Ay sir.

HIERONIMO   No sir, it was my murdered son,   80
O my son, my son, O my son Horatio!
But mine, or thine, Bazulto, be content.
Here, take my handkercher, and wipe thine eyes,
Whiles wretched I in thy mishaps may see
The lively portrait of my dying self.   85

He draweth out a bloody napkin

O no, not this: Horatio, this was thine,
And when I dyed it in thy dearest blood,
This was a token 'twixt thy soul and me
That of thy death revenged I should be.
But here, take this, and this – what, my purse? –   90
Ay, this, and that, and all of them are thine;
For all as one are our extremities.

1 CITIZEN

O see the kindness of Hieronimo!

2 CITIZEN

This gentleness shows him a gentleman.

HIERONIMO

See, see, O see thy shame, Hieronimo,   95
See here a loving father to his son!
Behold the sorrows and the sad laments
That he delivereth for his son's decease!
If love's effects so strives in lesser things,
If love enforce such moods in meaner wits,   100
If love express such power in poor estates –

77 *blood* passion
78-9 Shakespeare uses similar parallels (of sons who have lost fathers) in *Hamlet*.
Hieronimo's shame (see ll. 95 ff.) parallels Hamlet's after watching the First
Player act the tale of Priam.
80-1 lineation ed. (my murdred sonne, oh my sonne./My sonne . . . *Horatio. 1592*)
85 *lively* living
90 *this* this coin
92 *extremities* extreme sufferings
100 *meaner* of lower social rank

Hieronimo, whenas a raging sea
Tossed with the wind and tide, o'erturneth then
The upper billows, course of waves to keep,
Whilst lesser waters labour in the deep,   105
Then sham'st thou not, Hieronimo, to neglect
The sweet revenge of thy Horatio?
Though on this earth justice will not be found,
I'll down to hell, and in this passion
Knock at the dismal gates of Pluto's court,   110
Getting by force, as once Alcides did,
A troop of Furies and tormenting hags
To torture Don Lorenzo and the rest.
Yet lest the triple-headed porter should
Deny my passage to the slimy strond,   115
The Thracian poet thou shalt counterfeit:
Come on, old father, be my Orpheus,
And if thou canst no notes upon the harp,
Then sound the burden of thy sore heart's grief,
Till we do gain that Proserpine may grant   120

102–7 A difficult passage to explain. Hieronimo may mean that in storm conditions
(i.e. in a time of grief) the surface of the sea is driven into great waves (the
response of the 'upper waters' to the grief-storm), while other and less majestic
waters ('lesser waters') are troubled too. I think Hieronimo sees himself as, in
social standing, equivalent to the 'upper billows' and is ashamed he has not kept
his 'course of waves'; the Old Man has responded as lesser waters should. (For
an alternative explanation, reversing the roles, see Edwards). 'In the deep' need
not mean 'in the depths' but merely 'in the sea'.
102 *whenas* ed. (when as *1592*)
103 *o'erturneth* ed. (ore turnest *1592*)
109 *passion* suffering, deep emotion
110 *Pluto* god of the underworld
111 *Alcides* Heracles or Hercules, who in his twelfth labour descended to the
underworld and conquered Cerberus
114 *tripled-headed porter* the three-headed monstrous dog Cerberus, guardian of the
underworld
115 *slimy strond* See I, i, 27–9.
116 *Thracian poet* Orpheus (See next note.)
117 *Orpheus* The legendary poet and master of music who followed his dead wife
Eurydice to the underworld and induced Persephone (Proserpine) by his
playing to let her go. (See following lines.)
117–23 Hamilton (pp. 213–14) draws attention to the contrast between Orpheus'
mastery of art and song and his cruel experience of dismemberment at the hands
of the Bacchantes, thus reflecting the tension between the world of art and the
chaos of experience.
119 *burden* the theme or refrain of a song
120–1 The audience knows that Proserpine has already granted his request (I, i, 78
ff.).

Revenge on them that murdered my son.
Then will I rent and tear them thus and thus,
Shivering their limbs in pieces with my teeth.

Tear the papers

1 CITIZEN
O sir, my declaration!

Exit HIERONIMO *and they after*

2 CITIZEN
Save my bond!   125

Enter HIERONIMO

2 CITIZEN
Save my bond!
3 CITIZEN
Alas, my lease! it cost me ten pound,
And you, my lord, have torn the same.
HIERONIMO
That cannot be, I gave it never a wound;
Show me one drop of blood fall from the same: 130
How is it possible I should slay it then?
Tush, no; run after, catch me if you can.

Exeunt all but the OLD MAN

BAZULTO *remains till* HIERONIMO *enters again, who, staring*
him in the face, speaks

HIERONIMO
And art thou come, Horatio, from the depth,
To ask for justice in this upper earth?
To tell thy father thou art unrevenged,   135
To wring more tears from Isabella's eyes,
Whose lights are dimmed with over-long laments?
Go back my son, complain to Aeacus,
For here's no justice; gentle boy be gone,
For justice is exiled from the earth;   140
Hieronimo will bear thee company.
Thy mother cries on righteous Rhadamanth

122 *rent* rend
132 The similarity to Hamlet's behaviour after the killing of Polonius is striking
   (*Hamlet*, IV, ii). Hieronimo's mistaking the Old Man in the following lines is
   perhaps more acceptable to modern taste, as a way of expressing obsession, than
   Hamlet's vision of the Ghost in the Closet scene.
137 *lights* eyes
138 *Aeacus* a judge of the underworld. See I, i, 33.
142 *cries on* pleads to
142 *Rhadamanth* a judge of the underworld. See I, i, 33.

For just revenge against the murderers.
SENEX
Alas my lord, whence springs this troubled speech?
HIERONIMO
But let me look on my Horatio.   145
Sweet boy, how art thou changed in death's black shade!
Had Proserpine no pity on thy youth,
But suffered thy fair crimson-coloured spring
With withered winter to be blasted thus?
Horatio, thou art older than thy father;   150
Ah ruthless fate, that favour thus transforms!
SENEX
Ah my good lord, I am not your young son.
HIERONIMO
What, not my son? thou, then, a Fury art,
Sent from the empty kingdom of black night
To summon me to make appearance   155
Before grim Minos and just Rhadamanth,
To plague Hieronimo that is remiss,
And seeks not vengeance for Horatio's death.
SENEX
I am a grieved man, and not a ghost,
That came for justice for my murdered son.   160
HIERONIMO
Ay, now I know thee, now thou nam'st thy son;
Thou art the lively image of my grief:
Within thy face my sorrows I may see.
Thy eyes are gummed with tears, thy cheeks are wan,
Thy forehead troubled, and thy muttering lips   165
Murmur sad words abruptly broken off
By force of windy sighs thy spirit breathes;
And all this sorrow riseth for thy son:
And selfsame sorrow feel I for my son.
Come in old man, thou shalt to Isabel;   170
Lean on my arm: I thee, thou me shalt stay,
And thou, and I, and she, will sing a song,

149 *blasted* blighted
151 *fate* ed. (Father *1592*)
151 *favour* appearance, looks
153 *Fury* avenging spirit
156 *Minos* the third judge of the underworld. 'Grim' appears to contradict the
    estimate of Minos given at I, i, 50.
161 *thy* ed. (my *1592*)
162 *lively* living
171 *stay* sustain, prop up

Three parts in one, but all of discords framed –
Talk not of cords, but let us now be gone,
For with a cord Horatio was slain.   *Exeunt* 175

Act III, Scene xiv

Enter KING *of* SPAIN, *the* DUKE, VICEROY, *and* LORENZO,
BALTHAZAR, DON PEDRO, *and* BEL-IMPERIA

KING
Go brother, it is the Duke of Castile's cause,
Salute the viceroy in our name.
CASTILE   I go.
VICEROY
Go forth, Don Pedro, for thy nephew's sake,
And greet the Duke of Castile.
PEDRO   It shall be so.
KING
And now to meet these Portuguese,   5
For as we now are, so sometimes were these,
Kings and commanders of the western Indies.
Welcome, brave viceroy, to the court of Spain,
And welcome all his honourable train.
'Tis not unknown to us, for why you come,   10
Or have so kingly crossed the seas:
Sufficeth it, in this we note the troth
And more than common love you lend to us.
So is it that mine honourable niece,
(For it beseems us now that it be known)   15
Already is betrothed to Balthazar,
And by appointment and our condescent
To-morrow are they to be married.
To this intent we entertain thyself,

---

174 *cords* punning on the musical 'chord' and cord meaning rope
  1–2 lineation ed. (*as prose 1592*)
  6–7 Freeman (pp. 53–4) says that 'western Indies' here refers to Portuguese
      Brazil, a prize taken by Spain during the quarrels with Portugal of the late
      sixteenth century.
  9 *train* company, followers
  11 This looks like an absurd error, though Freeman (p. 12) suggests that the play
     may be set in Seville, frequently the seat of the Spanish court; in this case a
     Portuguese deputation might well travel partly by sea (via Cadiz).
  12 *troth* loyalty
  17 *condescent* agreement

Thy followers, their pleasure and our peace.   20
Speak, men of Portingale, shall it be so?
If ay, say so; if not, say flatly no.

VICEROY
Renowned king, I come not as thou think'st,
With doubtful followers, unresolved men,
But such as have upon thine articles   25
Confirmed thy motion and contented me.
Know sovereign, I come to solemnise
The marriage of thy beloved niece,
Fair Bel-imperia, with my Balthazar –
With thee, my son; whom sith I live to see,   30
Here take my crown, I give it her and thee;
And let me live a solitary life,
In ceaseless prayers,
To think how strangely heaven hath thee preserved.

KING
See brother, see, how nature strives in him!   35
Come, worthy viceroy, and accompany
Thy friend with thine extremities;
A place more private fits this princely mood.

VICEROY
Or here or where your highness thinks it good.
                              Exeunt all but CASTILE *and* LORENZO

CASTILE
Nay stay, Lorenzo, let me talk with you.   40
See'st thou this entertainment of these kings?

LORENZO
I do, my lord, and joy to see the same.

CASTILE
And knowest thou why this meeting is?

LORENZO
For her, my lord, whom Balthazar doth love,
And to confirm their promised marriage.   45

CASTILE
She is thy sister?

LORENZO   Who, Bel-imperia?
Ay, my gracious lord, and this is the day
That I have longed so happily to see.

20 *their* i.e. Bel-imperia and Balthazar

26 *motion* proposal

34 *strangely* wonderfully   35 *nature strives in him* he weeps

37 *extremities* extreme emotions

41 *entertainment* greeting, hospitable reception

46–8 lineation ed. (She ... Sister?/Who ... Lord,/And ... see. *1592*)

CASTILE
  Thou wouldst be loath that any fault of thine
  Should intercept her in her happiness.   50
LORENZO
  Heavens will not let Lorenzo err so much.
CASTILE
  Why then, Lorenzo, listen to my words:
  It is suspected and reported too,
  That thou, Lorenzo, wrong'st Hieronimo,
  And in his suits towards his majesty   55
  Still keep'st him back, and seeks to cross his suit.
LORENZO
  That I, my lord – ?
CASTILE
  I tell thee son, myself have heard it said,
  When, to my sorrow, I have been ashamed
  To answer for thee, though thou art my son.   60
  Lorenzo, knowest thou not the common love
  And kindness that Hieronimo hath won
  By his deserts within the court of Spain?
  Or seest thou not the king my brother's care
  In his behalf, and to procure his health?   65
  Lorenzo, shouldst thou thwart his passions,
  And he exclaim against thee to the king,
  What honour were't in this assembly,
  Or what a scandal were't among the kings
  To hear Hieronimo exclaim on thee?   70
  Tell me, and look thou tell me truly too,
  Whence grows the ground of this report in court?
LORENZO
  My lord, it lies not in Lorenzo's power
  To stop the vulgar, liberal of their tongues:
  A small advantage makes a water-breach,   75
  And no man lives that long contenteth all.
CASTILE
  Myself have seen thee busy to keep back
  Him and his supplications from the king.

50 *intercept* obstruct
56 *cross* interrupt, prevent
61 *common* widespread
66 *passions* laments, complaints
67 *exclaim against* denounce
74 *vulgar, liberal* ed. (vulgar liberall *1592*) common people, free with
75 *advantage* opportunity (for exploitation), weakness
75 *water-breach* a gap in wall or dyke caused by water-pressure

LORENZO

   Yourself, my lord, hath seen his passions,
   That ill beseemed the presence of a king;   80
   And for I pitied him in his distress,
   I held him thence with kind and courteous words,
   As free from malice to Hieronimo
   As to my soul, my lord.

CASTILE

   Hieronimo, my son, mistakes thee then.   85

LORENZO

   My gracious father, believe me so he doth.
   But what's a silly man, distract in mind,
   To think upon the murder of his son?
   Alas, how easy is it for him to err!
   But for his satisfaction and the world's,   90
   'Twere good, my lord, that Hieronimo and I
   Were reconciled, if he misconster me.

CASTILE

   Lorenzo, thou hast said; it shall be so;
   Go one of you and call Hieronimo.

Enter BALTHAZAR *and* BEL-IMPERIA

BALTHAZAR

   Come, Bel-imperia, Balthazar's content,   95
   My sorrow's ease and sovereign of my bliss,
   Sith heaven hath ordained thee to be mine;
   Disperse those clouds and melancholy looks,
   And clear them up with those thy sun-bright eyes,
   Wherein my hope and heaven's fair beauty lies.   100

BEL-IMPERIA

   My looks, my lord, are fitting for my love,
   Which new begun, can show no brighter yet.

BALTHAZAR

   New kindled flames should burn as morning sun.

BEL-IMPERIA

   But not too fast, lest heat and all be done.
   I see my lord my father.

---

80 *ill beseemed* fitted ill with
87 *silly* simple, poor
92 *misconster* misconstrue, wilfully misinterpret
102 *no brighter* ed. (brighter *1592*). *1594*'s emendation must be right; *1592* makes
   sense ('there's time for them to get brighter') but asks Bel-imperia to be coyly
   encouraging, an improbable attitude here.

BALTHAZAR   Truce, my love;   105
  I will go salute him.
CASTILE   Welcome, Balthazar,
  Welcome brave prince, the pledge of Castile's peace;
  And welcome Bel-imperia. How now, girl?
  Why com'st thou sadly to salute us thus?
  Content thyself, for I am satisfied;   110
  It is not now as when Andrea lived,
  We have forgotten and forgiven that,
  And thou art graced with a happier love.
  But Balthazar, here comes Hieronimo,
  I'll have a word with him.   115

            Enter HIERONIMO *and a* SERVANT

HIERONIMO
  And where's the duke?
SERVANT   Yonder.
HIERONIMO
                            Even so:
  What new device have they devised, trow?
  Pocas palabras! mild as the lamb,
  Is't I will be revenged? No, I am not the man.
CASTILE
  Welcome Hieronimo.   120
LORENZO
  Welcome Hieronimo.
BALTHAZAR
  Welcome Hieronimo.
HIERONIMO
  My lords, I thank you for Horatio.
CASTILE
  Hieronimo, the reason that I sent
  To speak with you, is this.
HIERONIMO   What, so short?   125

105–7 lineation ed. (I see ... Father./Truce ... him./Welcome .. Prince,/The ...
    peace: *1592*)
109 *sadly* with serious looks
110–13 This is yet another reference to the disapproval felt for Bel-imperia's liaison
    with Andrea (see I, i, 10–11 and note).
116–17 lineation ed. (*one line 1592*)
117–19 Hieronimo now feels threatened, like Hamlet later, by plots ('devices') on
    all sides.
117 *device* plot   117 *trow?* do you think?
118 *Pocas palabras* few words (Spanish)

Then I'll be gone, I thank you for't.

CASTILE

Nay, stay, Hieronimo – go call him, son.

LORENZO

Hieronimo, my father craves a word with you.

HIERONIMO

With me sir? why, my lord, I thought you had done.

LORENZO

[*Aside*] No, would he had.

CASTILE   Hieronimo, I hear   130

You find yourself aggrieved at my son

Because you have not access unto the king,

And say 'tis he that intercepts your suits.

HIERONIMO

Why, is not this a miserable thing, my lord?

CASTILE

Hieronimo, I hope you have no cause,   135

And would be loath that one of your deserts

Should once have reason to suspect my son,

Considering how I think of you myself.

HIERONIMO

Your son Lorenzo! whom, my noble lord?

The hope of Spain, mine honourable friend?   140

Grant me the combat of them, if they dare:

                              Draws out his sword

I'll meet him face to face, to tell me so.

These be the scandalous reports of such

As love not me, and hate my lord too much.

Should I suspect Lorenzo would prevent   145

Or cross my suit, that loved my son so well?

My lord, I am ashamed it should be said.

LORENZO

Hieronimo, I never gave you cause.

HIERONIMO

My good lord, I know you did not.

CASTILE   There then pause,

And for the satisfaction of the world,   150

128 s.p. LORENZO ed. (*not in 1592*)
130–1 lineation ed. (No, . . . had./Hieronimo . . . Sonne, *1592*)
133 *intercepts* obstructs, thwarts
141 *the combat of them* the right to meet them in (hand-to-hand) combat
144 *love* ed. (loues *1592*)
145 *prevent* forestall, obstruct
146 *cross* thwart
149–50 lineation ed. (There . . . world *one line 1592*)

Hieronimo, frequent my homely house,
The Duke of Castile, Cyprian's ancient seat,
And when thou wilt, use me, my son, and it.
But here, before Prince Balthazar and me,
Embrace each other, and be perfect friends.   155

HIERONIMO
Ay marry, my lord, and shall.
Friends, quoth he? see, I'll be friends with you all:
Specially with you, my lovely lord;
For divers causes it is fit for us
That we be friends – the world is suspicious,   160
And men may think what we imagine not.

BALTHAZAR
Why, this is friendly done, Hieronimo.

LORENZO
And thus I hope old grudges are forgot.

HIERONIMO
What else? it were a shame it should not be so.

CASTILE
Come on, Hieronimo, at my request;   165
Let us intreat your company today.
                    Exeunt [*all but* HIERONIMO]

HIERONIMO
Your lordship's to command. – Pha! keep your way:
Chi mi fa più carezze che non suole,
Tradito mi ha, o tradir vuole.   *Exit*

Act III, Scene xv

Ghost [*of* ANDREA] *and* REVENGE

ANDREA
Awake, Erichtho! Cerberus, awake!
Solicit Pluto, gentle Proserpine;

151 *homely* welcoming, hospitable, 'home-like'
153 *use* make use of, ask the services of
163 *thus* ed. (that *1592*)
167 *Pha!* an exclamation of contempt or disgust
168 *Chi . . . suole* ed. (*Mi. Chi mi fa? Pui Correzza Che non sule 1592*)
169 *Tradito . . . vuole* ed. (*Tradito viha otrade vule. 1592*)
168-9 'He who gives me more caresses than usual has betrayed me or wishes to
    betray me.'
  1 s.d. Ghost ed. (Enter *Ghoast 1592*)
  1 s.p. ANDREA ed. (*Ghost 1592 throughout this scene*)
  1 *Erichtho* ed. (*Erictha 1592*) 'the Thessalian sorceress' (Schick)

To combat, Acheron and Erebus!
For ne'er by Styx and Phlegethon in hell

. . . .   5

Nor ferried Charon to the fiery lakes
Such fearful sights, as poor Andrea sees!
Revenge, awake!

REVENGE
    Awake? for why?

ANDREA
    Awake, Revenge, for thou art ill-advised   10
    To sleep away what thou art warned to watch!

REVENGE
    Content thyself, and do not trouble me.

ANDREA
    Awake, Revenge, if love, as love hath had,
    Have yet the power or prevalence in hell!
    Hieronimo with Lorenzo is joined in league,   15
    And intercepts our passage to revenge:
    Awake, Revenge, or we are woe-begone!

3 *Acheron* ed. (*Achinon 1592*) See III, i, 55 and note.
3 *Erebus* ed. (*Ericus 1592*) primaeval darkness, child of chaos
4 *ne'er* ed. (neere *1592*)
4 *Styx and Phlegethon* rivers of the underworld
4 *in hell* (*end of l. 3 in 1592*)
6 *Charon* See I, i, 20 and note at I, i, 19.
7 *sees!* ed. (see? *1592*)
4-7 I accept Edwards's supposition that a line has dropped out after l. 4 (he
    suggests it might have been something like 'Was I distressed with outrage sore
    as this'). Only on this basis can the passage be made to give reasonable sense.
8 ff. The repetitions of 'Awake' may seem crude, and there is considerable
    suspicion that the text of this scene as a whole is a debased one (see Edwards,
    esp. pp. xxxiii and xxxviii–xxxix), yet the action does have dramatic point in
    giving emphatic expression to Andrea's sense that vengeance is becoming less
    and less probable – even Hieronimo seems to have betrayed the cause (see l. 15).
    Elizabethans would have understood the scene as referring to the 'worldling's'
    (see l. 18) faithless supposition that delay is equivalent to the abandoning of
    God's (or Revenge's) purposes. Revenge falling asleep was a familiar figure of
    the literature dealing with revenge.
11 *To sleep* ed. (Thsleep *1592*)
11 *away* ed. (away, *1592*). Edwards may be correct in accepting Hawkins's
    emendation 'awake!' in place of *1592*'s 'away'; but the text makes good sense as
    it stands and I see no compelling grounds for emendation.
11 *sleep away* sleep out
11 *watch* stay awake
14 *prevalence* ed. (preuailance *1592*)
17 *begone* ed. (degone *1592*)

REVENGE
    Thus worldlings ground, what they have dreamed, upon.
    Content thyself, Andrea: though I sleep,
    Yet is my mood soliciting their souls;   20
    Sufficeth thee that poor Hieronimo
    Cannot forget his son Horatio.
    Nor dies Revenge although he sleep awhile,
    For in unquiet, quietness is feigned,
    And slumbering is a common worldly wile.   25
    Behold, Andrea, for an instance how
    Revenge hath slept, and then imagine thou
    What 'tis to be subject to destiny.

Enter a Dumb Show [; they act and exeunt]

ANDREA
    Awake, Revenge, reveal this mystery.
REVENGE
    The two first, the nuptial torches bore,   30
    As brightly burning as the mid-day's sun;
    But after them doth Hymen hie as fast,
    Clothed in sable, and a saffron robe,
    And blows them out, and quencheth them with blood,
    As discontent that things continue so.   35
ANDREA
    Sufficeth me; thy meaning's understood;
    And thanks to thee and those infernal powers
    That will not tolerate a lover's woe.
    Rest thee, for I will sit to see the rest.
REVENGE
    Then argue not, for thou hast thy request.   40
                                    Exeunt

---

18 *worldlings ... upon* 'mortals base their beliefs on what they have merely dreamed (or fancied)'.
20 *mood* Edwards thinks 'anger' just possible; a more general sense such as 'attitude', 'purposes' seems required.
29 *reveal this mystery* explain the secret meaning of this action (the dumb show)
32 *Hymen* god of marriage
32 *hie* run
33 *sable* black
33 *saffron* yellow, the usual colour of Hymen's robe, here covered up with black

Act IV, Scene i

Enter BEL-IMPERIA *and* HIERONIMO

BEL-IMPERIA

Is this the love thou bear'st Horatio?
Is this the kindness that thou counterfeits?
Are these the fruits of thine incessant tears?
Hieronimo, are these thy passions,
Thy protestations and thy deep laments,   5
That thou wert wont to weary men withal?
O unkind father, O deceitful world!
With what excuses canst thou show thyself,
What what . . . .
From this dishonour and the hate of men?—   10
Thus to neglect the loss and life of him
Whom both my letters and thine own belief
Assures thee to be causeless slaughtered.
Hieronimo, for shame, Hieronimo,
Be not a history to after times   15
Of such ingratitude unto thy son.
Unhappy mothers of such children then –
But monstrous fathers, to forget so soon
The death of those, whom they with care and cost
Have tendered so, thus careless should be lost.   20
Myself a stranger in respect of thee,
So loved his life, as still I wish their deaths;
Nor shall his death be unrevenged by me,

---

4 *passions* passionate exclamations

7 *unkind* unnatural

9 *With what* ... ed. (With what dishonour, and the hate of men *1592*). The dots represent material presumed lost when the *1592* compositor inadvertently included in l. 9 the last six words of l. 10. The first two words (as printed) may be either the correct first words of the (now missing) l. 9 or a mistaken repeat of the beginning of l. 8. Bungling of some kind has certainly taken place, and since the true original cannot be recovered it seems best to indicate this by inserting dots.

15 *history* example, tale

17–20 An incomplete sentence; just plausible dramatically as reflecting in its lack of grammatical structure Bel-imperia's unsettled state of mind.

20 *tendered* cared for, cherished

21 *in respect of* compared to

Although I bear it out for fashion's sake:
For here I swear in sight of heaven and earth,   25
Shouldst thou neglect the love thou shouldst retain
And give it over and devise no more,
Myself should send their hateful souls to hell,
That wrought his downfall with extremest death.

HIERONIMO
But may it be that Bel-imperia   30
Vows such revenge as she hath deigned to say?
Why then, I see that heaven applies our drift
And all the saints do sit soliciting
For vengeance on those cursed murderers.
Madam 'tis true, and now I find it so;   35
I found a letter, written in your name,
And in that letter, how Horatio died.
Pardon, O pardon, Bel-imperia,
My fear and care in not believing it,
Nor think I thoughtless think upon a mean   40
To let his death be unrevenged at full;
And here I vow, so you but give consent,
And will conceal my resolution,
I will ere long determine of their deaths
That causeless thus have murdered my son.   45

BEL-IMPERIA
Hieronimo, I will consent, conceal;
And aught that may effect for thine avail
Join with thee to revenge Horatio's death.

HIERONIMO
On then; whatsoever I devise,
Let me entreat you, grace my practices.   50

24 *bear it ... sake* 'make a pretence of accepting the situation for the sake of appearances' (Edwards)
27 *devise* plot
29 *extremest* most cruel
32 *applies our drift* blesses our enterprise (drift, 'what we are driving at')
32 This is the outcome of Hieronimo's willingness to await 'opportunity' (see III, xiii, 27–8 and note).
39 *care* caution
40 *thoughtless* unconcerned
44 *determine of* bring about
47 *avail* assistance
50 *grace* support, involve yourself in

For why, the plot's already in mine head.
Here they are.

Enter BALTHAZAR *and* LORENZO

BALTHAZAR   How now, Hieronimo?
What, courting Bel-imperia?
HIERONIMO   Ay, my lord,
Such courting as, I promise you,
She hath my heart, but you, my lord, have hers.   55
LORENZO
But now, Hieronimo, or never,
We are to entreat your help.
HIERONIMO   My help?
Why, my good lords, assure yourselves of me,
For you have given me cause,
Ay, by my faith have you.
BALTHAZAR   It pleased you   60
At the entertainment of the ambassador
To grace the king so much as with a show:
Now were your study so well furnished,
As, for the passing of the first night's sport,
To entertain my father with the like,   65
Or any such-like pleasing motion,
Assure yourself it would content them well.
HIERONIMO
Is this all?
BALTHAZAR
Ay, this is all.
HIERONIMO
Why then I'll fit you; say no more.   70
When I was young I gave my mind
And plied myself to fruitless poetry:
Which though it profit the professor naught,
Yet is it passing pleasing to the world.

51 *For why* because
52–61 lineation ed. (Heere ... are./How ... Bel-Imperia./I ... you/She ...
hers./But ... helpe./My ... me./For ... you./It ... Embassadour. *1592*)
52 ff. Kyd here allows his actors an excellent opportunity for expressing, through
hypocritical politeness, the tensions between the three men.
62 *grace* honour
63 *furnished* stocked
66 *motion* entertainment
70 *I'll fit you* (a) 'I'll provide you what you need' (b) 'I'll pay you out' or 'I'll
punish you as you deserve' (Edwards)
73 *professor* the man who 'professes' or practises it

LORENZO
  And how for that?
HIERONIMO   Marry, my good lord, thus –   75
  And yet, methinks, you are too quick with us –
  When in Toledo there I studied,
  It was my chance to write a tragedy –
  See here my lords –   *He shows them a book*
  Which long forgot, I found this other day.   80
  Now would your lordships favour me so much
  As but to grace me with your acting it –
  I mean each one of you to play a part –
  Assure you it will prove most passing strange
  And wondrous plausible to that assembly.   85
BALTHAZAR
  What, would you have us play a tragedy?
HIERONIMO
  Why, Nero thought it no disparagement,
  And kings and emperors have ta'en delight
  To make experience of their wits in plays!
LORENZO
  Nay, be not angry good Hieronimo,   90
  The prince but asked a question.
BALTHAZAR
  In faith, Hieronimo, and you be in earnest,
  I'll make one.
LORENZO
  And I another.
HIERONIMO
  Now my good lord, could you entreat   95
  Your sister Bel-imperia to make one?
  For what's a play without a woman in it?
BEL-IMPERIA
  Little entreaty shall serve me, Hieronimo,
  For I must needs be employed in your play.

---

76 *too quick* too pressing; perhaps with a pun on quick meaning alive
76 unclear. Perhaps the line is meant to convey that Hieronimo's anger is only just
    under control.
84 *strange* remarkable, wonderful
85 *plausible* agreeable
87 *Nero* Hieronimo is correct in indicating that the Roman emperor Nero
    patronised plays and acted in them himself; at the same time he was associated
    with violence and deeds of blood, and the audience would no doubt pick up the
    allusion. Balthazar's nervousness (l. 155) is fully justified.
87 *disparagement* loss of dignity
89 *experience* trial   92 *and* if

HIERONIMO

Why, this is well; I tell you lordings,   100
It was determined to have been acted
By gentlemen and scholars too
Such as could tell what to speak.

BALTHAZAR

And now it shall be played by princes and courtiers,
Such as can tell how to speak,   105
If, as it is our country manner,
You will but let us know the argument.

HIERONIMO

That shall I roundly. The chronicles of Spain
Record this written of a knight of Rhodes:
He was betrothed, and wedded at the length   110
To one Perseda, an Italian dame,
Whose beauty ravished all that her beheld,
Especially the soul of Soliman,
Who at the marriage was the chiefest guest.
By sundry means sought Soliman to win   115
Perseda's love, and could not gain the same.
Then gan he break his passions to a friend,
One of his bashaws whom he held full dear;
Her had this bashaw long solicited,
And saw she was not otherwise to be won   120
But by her husband's death, this knight of Rhodes,
Whom presently by treachery he slew.
She, stirred with an exceeding hate therefore,

101 *determined* intended, arranged
103 *could tell* knew, were skilful
103–5 *what to speak... how to speak* not clear. Balthazar may mean only that courtiers are as skilled as 'gentlemen and scholars' in these matters. Some contrast may be intended between scholars who are good at invention and courtiers who are good at elocution.
107 *let us know the argument* Apparently we should think of the play as unscripted: Hieronimo will sketch in the plot and on that basis the actors will improvise their own lines. Kyd avoids repeating the 'argument' (or plot) by providing the King with a written copy (IV, iii, 6–7; IV, iv, 9–10). The 'abstracts' referred to at l. 141 would perhaps outline the play's narrative a little more fully.
107 *argument* plot, narrative
108 *roundly* plainly; at once
108–40 The playlet of Soliman and Perseda, as well as providing the mechanism of disaster, represents several of the main relationships of the larger play. See Introduction, pp. xxv–xxvi.
114 *was* ed. (way *1592*)
117 *break* disclose, confess
118 *bashaws* pashas, Turkish officers of high rank; courtiers

As cause of this slew Soliman;
And to escape the bashaw's tyranny   125
Did stab herself: and this the tragedy.

LORENZO
O excellent!

BEL-IMPERIA   But say, Hieronimo,
What then became of him that was the bashaw?

HIERONIMO
Marry thus: moved with remorse of his misdeeds,
Ran to a mountain-top and hung himself.   130

BALTHAZAR
But which of us is to perform that part?

HIERONIMO
O, that will I my lords, make no doubt of it:
I'll play the murderer, I warrant you,
For I already have conceited that.

BALTHAZAR
And what shall I?   135

HIERONIMO
Great Soliman the Turkish emperor.

LORENZO
And I?

HIERONIMO
Erastus the knight of Rhodes.

BEL-IMPERIA
And I?

HIERONIMO
Perseda, chaste and resolute.   140
And here, my lords, are several abstracts drawn,
For each of you to note your parts,
And act it, as occasion's offered you.
You must provide a Turkish cap,
A black mustachio and a fauchion.   145

Gives a paper to BALTHAZAR
You with a cross like to a knight of Rhodes.

Gives another to LORENZO
And madam, you must attire yourself

He giveth BEL-IMPERIA *another*

127-8 lineation ed. (O excellent./But ... him/That ... Bashaw? *1592*)
134 *conceited* envisaged, formed a conception of
141 *abstracts* outlines
141 *drawn* drawn up, written out
145 *fauchion* a broad curved sword (also spelled 'falchion')

Like Phoebe, Flora, or the Huntress,
Which to your discretion shall seem best.
And as for me, my lords, I'll look to one;   150
And, with the ransom that the viceroy sent
So furnish and perform this tragedy,
As all the world shall say Hieronimo
Was liberal in gracing of it so.
BALTHAZAR
Hieronimo, methinks a comedy were better.   155
HIERONIMO
A comedy?
Fie, comedies are fit for common wits:
But to present a kingly troop withal,
Give me a stately-written tragedy,
Tragedia cothurnata, fitting kings,   160
Containing matter, and not common things.
My lords, all this must be performed,
As fitting for the first night's revelling.
The Italian tragedians were so sharp of wit,
That in one hour's meditation   165
They would perform anything in action.
LORENZO
And well it may; for I have seen the like
In Paris, 'mongst the French tragedians.
HIERONIMO
In Paris? mass, and well remembered!
There's one thing more that rests for us to do.   170
BALTHAZAR
What's that, Hieronimo? forget not anything.

148 *Huntress* Diana, goddess of hunting
150 *look to* prepare
154 *gracing* setting it out, adorning it
156–7 lineation ed. (A . . . wits *one line 1592*)
158 *kingly troop* royal audience
160 *cothurnata* ed. (*cother nato 1592*)
160 *Tragedia cothurnata* in ancient Athens tragedy performed by an actor wearing buskins (thick-soled boots); the most serious kind of drama
161 *matter* substance, serious content
164–6 The reference is to the performers of the *Commedia dell' arte*, who improvised plays from scenarios.
170 *rests* remains

HIERONIMO

   Each one of us must act his part
   In unknown languages,
   That it may breed the more variety.
   As you, my lord, in Latin, I in Greek,   175
   You in Italian; and for because I know
   That Bel-imperia hath practised the French,
   In courtly French shall all her phrases be.

BEL-IMPERIA

   You mean to try my cunning then, Hieronimo.

BALTHAZAR

   But this will be a mere confusion,   180
   And hardly shall we all be understood.

HIERONIMO

   It must be so, for the conclusion
   Shall prove the invention and all was good.
   And I myself in an oration,
   And with a strange and wondrous show besides,   185
   That I will have there behind a curtain,
   Assure yourself, shall make the matter known.
   And all shall be concluded in one scene,
   For there's no pleasure ta'en in tediousness.

BALTHAZAR

   [*Aside to* LORENZO] How like you this?   190

LORENZO

   Why, thus my lord,
   We must resolve to soothe his humours up.

BALTHAZAR

   On then Hieronimo, farewell till soon.

172 ff. It is not clear whether the 'sundry languages' will ever have been used on
    stage. The note to the reader at IV, iv, 10 s.d. seems to suggest they were, and
    that the present text of the playlet is a translation, perhaps expanded, from the
    original. Since the audience has already heard the play's 'argument' they might
    well have been content to listen to 'unknown languages', provided they were not
    given too much of them and provided the action that accompanied them was
    highly explicit and stylised. Johnson (p. 24) makes a good case for supposing
    that 'sundry languages' were indeed used, without mystifying the audience.
173 *unknown* i.e. not in our own tongue
179 *cunning* skill
183 *invention* basic idea
185 *strange and wondrous show* Horatio's body: the emblem that justifies and
    explains the whole elaborate business.
185-6 transposed in *1592*
192 *We must resolve* (ends l. 191 in *1592*)
192 *soothe . . . up* indulge his whims

HIERONIMO
    You'll ply this gear?
LORENZO   I warrant you.
                              Exeunt all but HIERONIMO
HIERONIMO   Why so.
    Now shall I see the fall of Babylon,   195
    Wrought by the heavens in this confusion.
    And if the world like not this tragedy,
    Hard is the hap of old Hieronimo.   *Exit*

Act IV, Scene ii

Enter ISABELLA *with a weapon*

ISABELLA
    Tell me no more! O monstrous homicides!
    Since neither piety nor pity moves
    The king to justice or compassion,
    I will revenge myself upon this place
    Where thus they murdered my beloved son.   5
                              She cuts down the arbour
    Down with these branches and these loathsome boughs
    Of this unfortunate and fatal pine:
    Down with them, Isabella, rent them up
    And burn the roots from whence the rest is sprung.
    I will not leave a root, a stalk, a tree,   10

194 *ply this gear* carry out this business
194–5 lineation ed. (*one line in 1592*)
195 *fall of Babylon* Johnson (pp. 24 ff.) explains that the Geneva Bible (in use at
    Kyd's date of writing) uses 'Babel' both for the Tower of Babel and for the
    wicked city of Babylon: the two would be closely associated in the audience's
    mind. For the destruction of Babylon see Isaiah xiii, Jeremiah li and Revelation
    xviii. Elizabethans readily thought of Babylon as signifying Rome, and would
    therefore associate the reference with the King of Spain, in their eyes an agent
    of the Pope. Broude (pp. 143–5) argues that while the play's Spain cannot be
    taken as historical it is fully evocative of a depraved kingdom.
  1 s.p. ISABELLA ed. (*not in 1592*)
  5 s.d. Isabella may merely strip the leaves and branches from the arbour; or she
    may topple a property tree if one was used. See II, iv, 53 s.d. and note. Johnson
    (p. 26) sees Isabella's action as prefiguring 'the fall of Babylon', since the
    Hanging Gardens of Babylon were a wonder of the ancient world, and for her
    wickedness Babylon (or Babel) was laid desolate (for the Biblical references see
    the note to IV, i, 195 above).
  7 *unfortunate* ominous   8 *rent* rend, tear

A bough, a branch, a blossom, nor a leaf,
No, not an herb within this garden-plot.
Accursed complot of my misery,
Fruitless for ever may this garden be!
Barren the earth, and blissless whosoever   15
Imagines not to keep it unmanured!
An eastern wind commixed with noisome airs
Shall blast the plants and the young saplings;
The earth with serpents shall be pestered,
And passengers, for fear to be infect,   20
Shall stand aloof, and, looking at it, tell,
'There, murdered, died the son of Isabel.'
Ay, here he died, and here I him embrace:
See where his ghost solicits with his wounds
Revenge on her that should revenge his death.   25
Hieronimo, make haste to see thy son,
For sorrow and despair hath cited me
To hear Horatio plead with Rhadamanth:
Make haste, Hieronimo, to hold excused
Thy negligence in pursuit of their deaths,   30
Whose hateful wrath bereaved him of his breath.
Ah nay, thou dost delay their deaths,
Forgives the murderers of thy noble son,
And none but I bestir me – to no end.
And as I curse this tree from further fruit,   35
So shall my womb be cursed for his sake;
And with this weapon will I wound the breast,
                                        She stabs herself
The hapless breast that gave Horatio suck.   [*Exit*]

13 *complot* plot
16 *unmanured* uncultivated, barren
17 *noisome* pestilent
20 *passengers* passers-by
20 *infect* infected
27 *cited* summoned
28 *Rhadamanth* one of the judges of the underworld
29 *hold excused* to have it held excused
34 *me – to* ed. (me to *1592*)
32–4 Even Isabella is deceived by Hieronimo's plan of stealthy and circumspect
    revenge.
37 s.d., 38 s.d. The stage has to be cleared, though there is no one to remove
    Isabella's body. Presumably she stumbles off, wounded.

Act IV, Scene iii

Enter HIERONIMO; *he knocks up the curtain.*
Enter the DUKE OF CASTILE

CASTILE
  How now Hieronimo, where's your fellows,
  That you take all this pain?
HIERONIMO
  O sir, it is for the author's credit
  To look that all things may go well.
  But, good my lord, let me entreat your grace   5
  To give the king the copy of the play:
  This is the argument of what we show.
CASTILE
  I will, Hieronimo.
HIERONIMO
  One thing more, my good lord.
CASTILE
  What's that?   10
HIERONIMO
  Let me entreat your grace
  That, when the train are passed into the gallery,
  You would vouchsafe to throw me down the key.
CASTILE
  I will, Hieronimo.   *Exit* CASTILE
HIERONIMO
  What are you ready, Balthazar?   15
  Bring a chair and a cushion for the king.

Enter BALTHAZAR *with a chair*

1 s.d. Hieronimo probably hangs a curtain over one of the large entrance-doors at
   the rear of the Elizabethan stage. This permits the tableau of Horatio's body to
   be set up. Hattaway (p. 126) points out that this is the arrangement suggested
   by the German source-narrative. Rowan (pp. 122-3) suggests the cloth might
   be used to conceal the arbour, with the actor playing Isabella hidden behind it,
   who would then double as the body of Horatio.
1 *fellows* fellow actors
7 *argument* plot, narrative
12-13 It would seem natural to use the upper stage for the King and courtiers
     watching the play; subsequent action shows, however, that all the actors
     remained on the main stage. The 'gallery' must refer to the 'hall' or 'long
     gallery' of a large Elizabethan house. 'Throw down' is explained by Edwards as
     'throw the key down [on the floor] for me.'

Well done, Balthazar; hang up the title.
Our scene is Rhodes – what, is your beard on?

BALTHAZAR

Half on, the other is in my hand.

HIERONIMO

Despatch for shame, are you so long?   20

Exit BALTHAZAR

Bethink thyself, Hieronimo,
Recall thy wits, recompt thy former wrongs
Thou has received by murder of thy son;
And lastly, not least, how Isabel,
Once his mother and thy dearest wife,   25
All woe-begone for him, hath slain herself.
Behoves thee then, Hieronimo, to be revenged.
The plot is laid of dire revenge:
On then, Hieronimo, pursue revenge,
For nothing wants but acting of revenge.   30

Exit HIERONIMO

Act IV, Scene iv

Enter SPANISH KING, VICEROY, *the* DUKE OF CASTILE, *and their train*

KING

Now, Viceroy, shall we see the tragedy
Of Soliman the Turkish emperor,
Performed of pleasure by your son the prince,
My nephew Don Lorenzo, and my niece.

VICEROY

Who, Bel-imperia?   5

KING

Ay, and Hieronimo, our marshal,

17-18 *title . . . scene* There is some evidence that Elizabethan theatres used both title-boards and locality-labels to give audiences information they might otherwise miss.

18-19 *beard . . . Half on* Kyd deliberately, and with some finesse, makes the play-occasion as authentic as possible, and so provides the greatest degree of contrast between the surface normality and the horror to come: an intensification of the play's continuing irony.

20 *Despatch* hurry

22 *recompt* call to memory

3 *of pleasure* at their pleasure

At whose request they deign to do't themselves:
These be our pastimes in the court of Spain.
Here, brother, you shall be the book-keeper:
This is the argument of that they show.   10

He giveth him a book

Gentlemen, this play of Hieronimo, in sundry languages, was
thought good to be set down in English more largely, for the
easier understanding to every public reader.

Enter BALTHAZAR, BEL-IMPERIA, *and* HIERONIMO

BALTHAZAR

Bashaw, that Rhodes is ours, yield heavens the honour,
And holy Mahomet, our sacred prophet;
And be thou graced with every excellence
That Soliman can give, or thou desire.
But thy desert in conquering Rhodes is less   15
Than in reserving this fair Christian nymph,
Perseda, blissful lamp of excellence,
Whose eyes compel, like powerful adamant,
The warlike heart of Soliman to wait.

KING

See, Viceroy, that is Balthazar, your son,   20
That represents the emperor Soliman:
How well he acts his amorous passion.

VICEROY

Ay, Bel-imperia hath taught him that.

CASTILE

That's because his mind runs all on Bel-imperia.

HIERONIMO

Whatever joy earth yields betide your majesty.   25

BALTHAZAR

Earth yields no joy without Perseda's love.

HIERONIMO

Let then Perseda on your grace attend.

BALTHAZAR

She shall not wait on me, but I on her:

9 *book-keeper* in the Elizabethan theatre referring to the book-holder and
  prompter
10 s.d. See IV, 1, 172 ff. and note.
16 *reserving* preserving, protecting
18 *adamant* the loadstone (which had magnetic properties)
19 *wait* attend on her
20–4 Kyd takes some pains to see that the audience is aware of the parallels
  between the actor and his assumed part.

Drawn by the influence of her lights, I yield.
But let my friend, the Rhodian knight, come forth,   30
Erasto, dearer than my life to me,
That he may see Perseda, my beloved.

Enter [LORENZO *as*] ERASTO

KING
  Here comes Lorenzo; look upon the plot,
  And tell me, brother, what part plays he?
BEL-IMPERIA
  Ah, my Erasto, welcome to Perseda.   35
LORENZO
  Thrice happy is Erasto that thou liv'st –
  Rhodes' loss is nothing to Erasto's joy;
  Sith his Perseda lives, his life survives.
BALTHAZAR
  Ah, bashaw, here is love between Erasto
  And fair Perseda, sovereign of my soul.   40
HIERONIMO
  Remove Erasto, mighty Soliman,
  And then Perseda will be quickly won.
BALTHAZAR
  Erasto is my friend, and while he lives
  Perseda never will remove her love.
HIERONIMO
  Let not Erasto live to grieve great Soliman.   45
BALTHAZAR
  Dear is Erasto in our princely eye.
HIERONIMO
  But if he be your rival, let him die.
BALTHAZAR
  Why, let him die: so love commandeth me.
  Yet grieve I that Erasto should so die.
HIERONIMO
  Erasto, Soliman saluteth thee,   50
  And lets thee wit by me his highness' will
  Which is, thou shouldst be thus employed.
                                                      Stab him
BEL-IMPERIA   *Ay me,*
  Erasto! see, Soliman, Erasto's slain!

29 *lights* eyes
33 *plot* synopsis and cast-list
37 *to* compared to
52 *Ay me,* ed. (*begins l. 53 in 1592*)

BALTHAZAR

    Yet liveth Soliman to comfort thee.
    Fair queen of beauty, let not favour die,   55
    But with a gracious eye behold his grief,
    That with Perseda's beauty is increased,
    If by Perseda his grief be not released.

BEL-IMPERIA

    Tyrant, desist soliciting vain suits;
    Relentless are mine ears to thy laments,   60
    As thy butcher is pitiless and base,
    Which seized on my Erasto, harmless knight,
    Yet by thy power thou thinkest to command,
    And to thy power Perseda doth obey:
    But were she able, thus she would revenge   65
    Thy treacheries on thee, ignoble prince: *Stab him*
    And on herself she would be thus revenged.   *Stab herself*

KING

    Well said, old marshal, this was bravely done!

HIERONIMO

    But Bel-imperia plays Perseda well.

VICEROY

    Were this in earnest, Bel-imperia,   70
    You would be better to my son than so.

KING

    But now what follows for Hieronimo?

HIERONIMO

    Marry, this follows for Hieronimo:
    Here break we off our sundry languages
    And thus conclude I in our vulgar tongue.   75
    Haply you think, but bootless are your thoughts,
    That this is fabulously counterfeit,
    And that we do as all tragedians do:
    To die today, for fashioning our scene,
    The death of Ajax, or some Roman peer,   80

55 *favour* i.e. your love
58 *Perseda his* ed. (Persedaes 1592). 'His' must be heavily elided, as the *1592* spelling indicates.
68 *Well said* The King refers to Hieronimo's success in composing the piece: 'Well done'.
75 *vulgar tongue* the vernacular, our everyday speech
76–86 The fiction–fact relationship, stated very simply here by Kyd, became a topic for much more subtle exploration by Shakespeare and later Elizabethan dramatists.   76 *Haply* perhaps
76 *bootless* unavailing   77 *fabulously counterfeit* acted in fiction only
79 *for ... scene* ed. (for (fashioning our scene) *1592*) enacting our play

And in a minute starting up again,
Revive to please to-morrow's audience.
No, princes; know I am Hieronimo,
The hopeless father of a hapless son,
Whose tongue is tuned to tell his latest tale,   85
Not to excuse gross errors in the play.
I see your looks urge instance of these words;
Behold the reason urging me to this:

Shows his dead son

See here my show, look on this spectacle.
Here lay my hope, and here my hope hath end;   90
Here lay my heart, and here my heart was slain;
Here lay my treasure, here my treasure lost;
Here lay my bliss, and here my bliss bereft;
But hope, heart, treasure, joy, and bliss,
All fled, failed, died, yea, all decayed with this.   95
From forth these wounds came breath that gave me life;
They murdered me that made these fatal marks.
The cause was love, whence grew this mortal hate,
The hate, Lorenzo and young Balthazar,
The love, my son to Bel-imperia.   100
But night, the coverer of accursed crimes,
With pitchy silence hushed these traitors' harms
And lent them leave, for they had sorted leisure
To take advantage in my garden-plot
Upon my son, my dear Horatio: 105
There merciless they butchered up my boy,
In black dark night, to pale dim cruel death.
He shrieks, I heard, and yet methinks I hear,
His dismal outcry echo in the air.
With soonest speed I hasted to the noise,   110
Where hanging on a tree I found my son,
Through-girt with wounds, and slaughtered as you see.
And grieved I, think you, at this spectacle?
Speak, Portuguese, whose loss resembles mine:
If thou canst weep upon thy Balthazar,   115
'Tis like I wailed for my Horatio.
And you, my lord, whose reconciled son

85 *latest* last   87 *instance* explanation, what lies behind (these words)
89 *show* tableau, spectacle

96 *From forth . . . life* i.e. *my* life-breath left me when these wounds were made in
    my son's body.   102 *harms* their malicious actions
103 *sorted* sought out   112 *Through-girt* pierced through
117 *reconciled* presumably to Hieronimo. See III, xiv, 130–64.

Marched in a net, and thought himself unseen
And rated me for brainsick lunacy,
With 'God amend that mad Hieronimo!' –   120
How can you brook our play's catastrophe?
And here behold this bloody handkercher,
Which at Horatio's death I weeping dipped
Within the river of his bleeding wounds:
It as propitious, see I have reserved,   125
And never hath it left my bloody heart,
Soliciting remembrance of my vow
With these, O these accursed murderers:
Which now performed, my heart is satisfied.
And to this end the bashaw I became   130
That might revenge me on Lorenzo's life,
Who therefore was appointed to the part,
And was to represent the knight of Rhodes,
That I might kill him more conveniently.
So, Viceroy, was this Balthazar, thy son –   135
That Soliman which Bel-imperia
In person of Perseda murdered –
Solely appointed to that tragic part
That she might slay him that offended her.
Poor Bel-imperia missed her part in this: 140
For though the story saith she should have died,
Yet I of kindness, and of care to her,
Did otherwise determine of her end;
But love of him whom they did hate too much
Did urge her resolution to be such.   145
And princes, now behold Hieronimo,
Author and actor in this tragedy,
Bearing his latest fortune in his fist:
And will as resolute conclude his part
As any of the actors gone before.   150
And, gentles, thus I end my play:
Urge no more words: I have no more to say.

He runs to hang himself

118 *Marched in a net* kept himself concealed, practised deceit; a proverbial phrase
119 *rated* berated
119–20 Compare Lorenzo's advice to the King at III, xii, 85–9 and 96–8.
125 *propitious* of good omen; a token prompting to due revenge
130–52 This may be over-explicit; but audiences are notoriously slow at registering
    the action of plays, especially when they have more than one group of actors to
    watch, as is the case with Hieronimo's playlet and its audience.
140 *missed her part* strayed from her assigned part

KING

O hearken, Viceroy! Hold, Hieronimo!
Brother, my nephew and thy son are slain!

VICEROY

We are betrayed! my Balthazar is slain!   155
Break ope the doors, run, save Hieronimo.
[They break in, and hold HIERONIMO]
Hieronimo, do but inform the king of these events;
Upon mine honour thou shalt have no harm.

HIERONIMO

Viceroy, I will not trust thee with my life,
Which I this day have offered to my son.   160
Accursed wretch,
Why stayest thou him that was resolved to die?

KING

Speak, traitor; damned, bloody murderer, speak!
For now I have thee I will make thee speak –
Why hast thou done this undeserving deed?   165

VICEROY

Why hast thou murdered my Balthazar?

CASTILE

Why hast thou butchered both my children thus?

HIERONIMO

O, good words!
As dear to me was my Horatio
As yours, or yours, or yours, my lord, to you.   170
My guiltless son was by Lorenzo slain,

---

153 *Hold, Hieronimo!* ed. (holde *Hieronimo*, *1592*) wait, Hieronimo; 'hold' in *1592*
    might mean 'arrest'.
156 The doors have been locked by Castile, as Hieronimo requested (IV, iii, 12–13).
    The attendants 'break in' from off-stage and guard Hieronimo.
161 *Accursed wretch*, ed. (*begins l. 162 in 1592*)
165–7 and 179–82 Edwards finds the questions at these points an 'extraordinary
    inconsistency', since Hieronimo has already 'told [the king] everything'. He
    accounts for the inconsistency by supposing (with Schücking) that IV, iv,
    153–201 represents 'an alternative ending to the play', replacing Hieronimo's
    long speech (ll. 73–152), and requiring therefore the brief explanation at ll. 169
    ff. Edwards makes out a good case, but the inconsistency may be less glaring
    than at first appears, for at l. 179 the King is asking Hieronimo to discuss his
    confederates (Bel-imperia principally), which he has not yet done in detail;
    Hieronimo refuses to break the vow he swore to Bel-imperia at IV, i, 42–5 (see
    ll. 187–8). The King's earlier questioning, and that of the Viceroy and Castile,
    might be explained as the result of grief-stricken bewilderment and not mere
    redundancy; they have not taken in what Hieronimo has said.
168 *O, good words* ed. (*begins l. 169 in 1592*)

And by Lorenzo and that Balthazar
Am I at last revenged thoroughly,
Upon whose souls may heavens be yet avenged
With greater far than these afflictions.   175

CASTILE
But who were thy confederates in this?

VICEROY
That was thy daughter Bel-imperia;
For by her hand my Balthazar was slain:
I saw her stab him.

KING   Why speak'st thou not?

HIERONIMO
What lesser liberty can kings afford   180
Than harmless silence? Then afford it me:
Sufficeth I may not, nor I will not tell thee.

KING
Fetch forth the tortures.
Traitor as thou art, I'll make thee tell.

HIERONIMO   Indeed,
Thou may'st torment me, as his wretched son   185
Hath done in murdering my Horatio,
But never shalt thou force me to reveal
The thing which I have vowed inviolate.
And therefore in despite of all thy threats,
Pleased with their deaths, and eased with their revenge,   190
First take my tongue, and afterwards my heart.
                              [*He bites out his tongue*]

KING
O monstrous resolution of a wretch!
See, Viceroy, he hath bitten forth his tongue
Rather than to reveal what we required.

CASTILE
Yet can he write.   195

KING
And if in this he satisfy us not,
We will devise th'extremest kind of death

172 *by* i.e. by the deaths of
184 *Indeed* ed. (*begins l. 185 in 1592*)
191 s.d. Barish (p.82) thinks this section 'betrays the final despair at the uselessness
of talk, the beserk resolve to have done with language forever.' Johnson (p. 34)
says it 'serves to identify Hieronimo as admirably stoic' since his action imitates
Zeno of Elea, the famous Stoic, who under torture 'bit off his own tongue, and
spat it out in the tormentor's face' (quoting William Baldwin's *Treatise of
Morall Philosophie*, 9th ed., 1579).

That ever was invented for a wretch.
                    Then he makes signs for a knife to mend his pen
CASTILE
O, he would have a knife to mend his pen.
VICEROY
Here; and advise thee that thou write the troth.   200
KING
Look to my brother! save Hieronimo!
                    He with a knife stabs the DUKE *and himself*
What age hath ever heard such monstrous deeds?
My brother, and the whole succeeding hope
That Spain expected after my decease!
Go bear his body hence, that we may mourn   205
The loss of our beloved brother's death;
That he may be entombed, whate'er befall:
I am the next, the nearest, last of all.
VICEROY
And thou, Don Pedro, do the like for us;
Take up our hapless son, untimely slain: 210
Set me with him, and he with woeful me,
Upon the main-mast of a ship unmanned,
And let the wind and tide haul me along
To Scylla's barking and untamed gulf,
Or to the loathsome pool of Acheron,   215
To weep my want for my sweet Balthazar:
Spain hath no refuge for a Portingale.

The trumpets sound a dead march, the KING *of* SPAIN
mourning after his brother's body, and the VICEROY *of*
PORTINGALE *bearing the body of his son*

200 *advise thee* be advised, take care
201 s.p. KING ed. (*not in 1592*)
202–4 Patriotic feelings may be involved here: English audiences would be delighted
    by Spain's discomfiture. Hill *passim* makes the destruction of the Spanish
    succession a central preoccupation of the play.
213 *haul* drive; hale; possibly, suggests Edwards, a word with nautical associations
    for Kyd
214 *gulf* ed. (greefe *1592*)
214 *Scylla's ... gulf* Scylla was one of a pair of dangerous rocks (the other was
    Charybdis) between Italy and Sicily; Joseph says that Homer refers to Scylla,
    the goddess of the rock, as 'barking', while later writers described her as
    accompanied by barking dogs.
215 *Acheron* See I, i, 19 and note.
216 *my want for* my loss of
217 s.d. VICEROY OF PORTINGALE ed. (*King of Portingale 1592*)

Act IV, Scene v

Ghost [of ANDREA] *and* REVENGE

ANDREA
Ay, now my hopes have end in their effects,
When blood and sorrow finish my desires:
Horatio murdered in his father's bower,
Vild Serberine by Pedringano slain,
False Pedringano hanged by quaint device,   5
Fair Isabella by herself misdone,
Prince Balthazar by Bel-imperia stabbed,
The Duke of Castile and his wicked son
Both done to death by old Hieronimo,
My Bel-imperia fallen as Dido fell,   10
And good Hieronimo slain by himself:
Ay, these were spectacles to please my soul.
Now will I beg at lovely Proserpine,
That, by the virtue of her princely doom,
I may consort my friends in pleasing sort,   15
And on my foes work just and sharp revenge.
I'll lead my friend Horatio through those fields
Where never-dying wars are still inured:
I'll lead fair Isabella to that train
Where pity weeps but never feeleth pain: 20
I'll lead my Bel-imperia to those joys
That vestal virgins and fair queens possess;

1 s.d. *Ghost* ed. (*Enter Ghoast 1592*)
1 s.p. ANDREA ed. (*Ghoast. 1592 throughout this scene*)
1–2 Compare I, v, II, vi and III, xv, 29–40. Adams argues that Andrea's interest in
     the action throughout is largely aesthetic in character; he is now satisfied that a
     dramatically coherent action has worked itself out.
4 *Vild* vile
5 *quaint* cunning
6 *misdone* slain
10 *as Dido fell* Virgil (*Aeneid* IV) records that Dido killed herself after Aeneas's
    departure from Carthage. The legend Virgil adapted also speaks of Dido as a
    suicide, killing herself to avoid marriage with Iarbas.
14 *doom* judgment
15 *consort* accompany, treat
18 *inured* carried on
19 *train* company
22 *vestal virgins* virgins consecrated to the Roman goddess Vesta, and vowed to
    chastity

I'll lead Hieronimo where Orpheus plays,
Adding sweet pleasure to eternal days.
But say, Revenge, for thou must help, or none,   25
Against the rest how shall my hate be shown?

REVENGE

This hand shall hale them down to deepest hell,
Where none but Furies, bugs and tortures dwell.

ANDREA

Then, sweet Revenge, do this at my request;
Let me be judge, and doom them to unrest: 30
Let loose poor Tityus from the vulture's gripe,
And let Don Cyprian supply his room;
Place Don Lorenzo on Ixion's wheel,
And let the lover's endless pains surcease –
Juno forgets old wrath, and grants him ease;   35
Hang Balthazar about Chimaera's neck,
And let him there bewail his bloody love,
Repining at our joys that are above;
Let Serberine go roll the fatal stone,
And take from Sisyphus his endless moan;   40
False Pedringano for his treachery,
Let him be dragged through boiling Acheron,
And there live, dying still in endless flames,
Blaspheming gods and all their holy names.

REVENGE

Then haste we down to meet thy friends and foes: 45
To place thy friends in ease, the rest in woes.
For here, though death hath end their misery,
I'll there begin their endless tragedy.   *Exeunt*

---

23 *Orpheus* See III, xiii, 117 and note.   28 *bugs* bugbears, horrors
32 *Don Cyprian* The Duke of Castile; he had frowned on Andrea's relationship
   with Bel-imperia (see II, i, 45–8).
32 *supply his room* take his place
34 *the lover* Ixion, who had tried to seduce Juno.
34 *surcease* cease
36 *Chimaera* a fire-breathing monster of Greek mythology, with head of a lion,
   body of a goat, tail of a dragon
40 *Sisyphus* a legendary king of Crete, condemned for his misdeeds to roll a large
   stone eternally uphill in the underworld
43 *still* continually, for ever
45–8 Adams sees these lines as Revenge's way of ensuring that an *aesthetic*
   response to the events we have witnessed is the dominant one; whatever the
   actuality of posthumous experience for these people, it will form part, properly
   understood, of their (aesthetically understood) 'tragedy', though that tragedy
   being 'endless' is at odds with the canons of art.
47 *end* ended

Scenes added to
THE SPANISH TRAGEDY
in the edition of 1602

First Addition, between II, v, 45 and 46 (p. 45)

[For outrage fits our cursed wretchedness.]
Ay me, Hieronimo, sweet husband speak.
HIERONIMO
He supped with us tonight, frolic and merry,
And said he would go visit Balthazar
At the duke's palace: there the prince doth lodge.
He had no custom to stay out so late,   5
He may be in his chamber; some go see.
Roderigo, ho!

Enter PEDRO *and* JAQUES

ISABELLA
Ay me, he raves. Sweet Hieronimo!
HIERONIMO
True, all Spain takes note of it.
Besides, he is so generally beloved   10
His majesty the other day did grace him
With waiting on his cup: these be favours
Which do assure he cannot be short-lived.
ISABELLA
Sweet Hieronimo!
HIERONIMO
I wonder how this fellow got his clothes?   15
Sirrah, sirrah, I'll know the truth of all:
Jaques, run to the Duke of Castile's presently,
And bid my son Horatio to come home:
I and his mother have had strange dreams tonight.
Do you hear me, sir?
JAQUES   Ay, sir.

2 *frolic* frolicsome, gay
7 *Roderigo, ho!* (*ends l. 6 in 1602*)
10 *generally* by everyone
11–12 See I, iv, 130.
13 *assure* ensure, prove
13 *he* ed. (me *1602*)
17 *presently* at once

HIERONIMO   Well sir, begone.   20
  Pedro, come hither: knowest thou who this is?
PEDRO
  Too well, sir.
HIERONIMO
  Too well? Who? Who is it? Peace, Isabella:
  Nay, blush not, man.
PEDRO   It is my lord Horatio.
HIERONIMO
  Ha, ha! Saint James, but this doth make me laugh,   25
  That there are more deluded than myself.
PEDRO
  Deluded?
HIERONIMO
  Ay, I would have sworn myself within this hour
  That this had been my son Horatio,
  His garments are so like.   30
  Ha! are they not great persuasions?
ISABELLA
  O, would to God it were not so!
HIERONIMO
  Were not, Isabella? Dost thou dream it is?
  Can thy soft bosom entertain a thought
  That such a black deed of mischief should be done   35
  On one so pure and spotless as our son?
  Away, I am ashamed.
ISABELLA   Dear Hieronimo,
  Cast a more serious eye upon thy grief:
  Weak apprehension gives but weak belief.
HIERONIMO
  It was a man, sure, that was hanged up here;   40
  A youth, as I remember: I cut him down.
  If it should prove my son now after all –
  Say you, say you, light! Lend me a taper,
  Let me look again. O God!
  Confusion, mischief, torment, death and hell,   45
  Drop all your stings at once in my cold bosom,
  That now is stiff with horror; kill me quickly:

20–4 lineation ed. (*prose in 1602*)
30–1 lineation ed. (*one line 1602*)
31 *persuasions* evidences, means of persuasion
36 *pure* ed. (poore *1602*)
37 *Dear Hieronimo* ed. (*begins l. 38 in 1602*)
39 *apprehension* understanding, grasp of what's happening
44 *O God!* ed. (*begins l. 45 in 1602*)

Be gracious to me, thou infective night,
And drop this deed of murder down on me;
Gird in my waste of grief with thy large darkness, 50
And let me not survive to see the light
May put me in the mind I had a son.

ISABELLA

O, sweet Horatio. O, my dearest son!

HIERONIMO

How strangely had I lost my way to grief!
[Sweet lovely rose, ill plucked before thy time,]

Second Addition, replacing III, ii, 65 and part of 66 (p. 55)

[LORENZO
Why so, Hieronimo? use me.]

HIERONIMO

Who, you, my lord?
I reserve your favour for a greater honour;
This is a very toy my lord, a toy.

LORENZO

All's one, Hieronimo, acquaint me with it.

HIERONIMO

I'faith, my lord, 'tis an idle thing. 5
I must confess, I ha' been too slack,
Too tardy. Too remiss unto your honour.

LORENZO

How now, Hieronimo?

HIERONIMO

In troth, my lord, it is a thing of nothing,
The murder of a son, or so: 10
A thing of nothing, my lord.

[LORENZO   Why then, farewell.]

48 *infective* bearing infection
50 *Gird in* confine, limit
50 *waste* a vast, empty area (with a play on 'waist')
 3 *toy* trifle, trivial thing
 5–7 lineation ed. (*prose in 1602*)

Third Addition, between III, xi, 1 and 2 (p. 79)

[1 PORTINGALE
  By your leave, sir.]
HIERONIMO
  'Tis neither as you think, nor as you think,
  Nor as you think: you're wide all:
  These slippers are not mine, they were my son Horatio's.
  My son, and what's a son? A thing begot
  Within a pair of minutes, thereabout: 5
  A lump bred up in darkness, and doth serve
  To ballace these light creatures we call women;
  And, at nine moneths' end, creeps forth to light.
  What is there yet in a son
  To make a father dote, rave or run mad?   10
  Being born, it pouts, cries, and breeds teeth.
  What is there yet in a son? He must be fed,
  Be taught to go, and speak. Ay, or yet?
  Why might not a man love a calf as well?
  Or melt in passion o'er a frisking kid,   15
  As for a son? Methinks a young bacon
  Or a fine little smooth horse-colt
  Should move a man as much as doth a son:
  For one of these in very little time
  Will grow to some good use, whereas a son,   20
  The more he grows in stature and in years,
  The more unsquared, unbevelled he appears,
  Reckons his parents among the rank of fools,
  Strikes care upon their heads with his mad riots,
  Makes them look old before they meet with age: 25
  This is a son:
  And what a loss were this, considered truly?
  Oh, but my Horatio

2 *wide* wide of the mark, quite wrong
4 *A thing begot* ed. (*begins l. 5 in 1602*)
7 *ballace* ballast, weigh down
8 *moneths* months (metre requires a dissyllable)
11 *breeds teeth* cuts teeth
13 *go* walk
13 *Ay, or yet?* Hieronimo means 'Yes, or what else?', 'What can I add?'
16 *young bacon* piglet
22 *unsquared, unbevelled* Boas says 'uneven and unpolished': the author of this
   Addition has in mind the rough manners of young bloods. 'Bevelling' is a
   decorative process in carpentry performed with a 'bevel' or 'bevel-square'.
26-30 lineation ed. (This ... truly./O ... of these/Insatiate ... parents, *1602*)

Grew out of reach of these insatiate humours:
He loved his loving parents,   30
He was my comfort, and his mother's joy,
The very arm that did hold up our house:
Our hopes were stored up in him,
None but a damned murderer could hate him.
He had not seen the back of nineteen year,   35
When his strong arm unhorsed the proud Prince Balthazar,
And his great mind, too full of honour,
Took him unto mercy,
That valiant but ignoble Portingale.
Well, heaven is heaven still,   40
And there is Nemesis and Furies,
And things called whips,
And they sometimes do meet with murderers:
They do not always 'scape, that's some comfort.
Ay, ay, ay, and then time steals on: 45
And steals, and steals, till violence leaps forth
Like thunder wrapped in a ball of fire,
And so doth bring confusion to them all.
[Good leave have you: nay, I pray you go,]

Fourth Addition, between III, xii and xiii (p. 85)

Enter JAQUES *and* PEDRO

JAQUES
I wonder, Pedro, why our master thus
At midnight sends us with our torches' light,
When man and bird and beast are all at rest,
Save those that watch for rape and bloody murder?

29 *insatiate humours* unsatisfied whims and caprices
35 *the back of* i.e. he was still nineteen
36–9 The syntax is unclear at this point. Presumably l. 39 simply expands 'the
    proud Prince Balthazar' (l. 36). Should l. 39 follow l. 36 immediately?
38 *unto* ed. (vs to *1602*)
38–9 lineation ed. (*one line 1602*)
41 *Nemesis* a personification of the gods' anger at human presumption, and their
    punishment of it
41 *Furies* legendary avengers of crime in ancient Greece
45–7 lineation ed. (I,... steales, and   steales/Till ... thunder/Wrapt ... fire,
    1602)
48 *confusion* destruction

PEDRO

  O Jaques, know thou that our master's mind   5
  Is much distraught since his Horatio died,
  And now his aged years should sleep in rest,
  His heart in quiet; like a desperate man,
  Grows lunatic and childish for his son:
  Sometimes, as he doth at his table sit,   10
  He speaks as if Horatio stood by him;
  Then starting in a rage, falls on the earth,
  Cries out 'Horatio, where is my Horatio?'
  So that with extreme grief and cutting sorrow,
  There is not left in him one inch of man: 15
  See, where he comes.

Enter HIERONIMO

HIERONIMO

  I pry through every crevice of each wall,
  Look on each tree, and search through every brake,
  Beat at the bushes, stamp our grandam earth,
  Dive in the water, and stare up to heaven,   20
  Yet cannot I behold my son Horatio.
  How now, who's there, sprites, sprites?

PEDRO

  We are your servants that attend you, sir.

HIERONIMO

  What make you with your torches in the dark?

PEDRO

  You bid us light them, and attend you here.   25

HIERONIMO

  No, no, you are deceived, not I, you are deceived:
  Was I so mad to bid you light your torches now?
  Light me your torches at the mid of noon,
  Whenas the sun-god rides in all his glory:
  Light me your torches then.

PEDRO   Then we burn daylight.   30

HIERONIMO

  Let it be burnt: night is a murderous slut,

12 *starting* starting up
17 *crevice* (creuie *1602*)
18 *brake* thicket
22 *sprites, sprites?* ed. (sprits, sprits? *1602*) spirits, demons
24 *What make you* What are you doing? What is your purpose?
29 *Whenas* when
30 *burn daylight* a phrase meaning to waste time; here used also in the literal sense

That would not have her treasons to be seen;
And yonder pale-faced Hecate there, the moon,
Doth give consent to that is done in darkness;
And all those stars that gaze upon her face,   35
Are aglets on her sleeve, pins on her train;
And those that should be powerful and divine,
Do sleep in darkness when they most should shine.

PEDRO
Provoke them not, fair sir, with tempting words:
The heavens are gracious, and your miseries   40
And sorrow makes you speak you know not what.

HIERONIMO
Villain, thou liest, and thou doest naught
But tell me I am mad: thou liest, I am not mad.
I know thee to be Pedro, and he Jaques.
I'll prove it to thee, and were I mad, how could I?   45
Where was she that same night when my Horatio
Was murdered? She should have shone: search thou the
    book.
Had the moon shone, in my boy's face there was a kind of
    grace,
That I know (nay, I do know) had the murderer seen him,
His weapon would have fallen and cut the earth,   50
Had he been framed of naught but blood and death.
Alack, when mischief doth it knows not what,
What shall we say to mischief?

                            Enter ISABELLA

ISABELLA
Dear Hieronimo, come in a-doors.
O, seek not means so to increase thy sorrow.   55

HIERONIMO
Indeed, Isabella, we do nothing here;

33 *Hecate* ed. (Hee-cat *1602*) In Greek thought a goddess associated with night
    and the lower world; Elizabethans associated her with the moon. Here, two
    syllables only.
36 *aglets* ed. (aggots *1602*) spangles ('properly, the ornamental tags of laces',
    Edwards)
36 *pins* spangles, ornaments
41 *And sorrow* ed. (*ends l. 40 in 1602*)
45 *prove it* I.e. prove the Heavens negligent in the matter of Horatio's murder.
47 *Was murdered* ed. (*ends l. 46 in 1602*)
47 *book* almanac, recording the phases of the moon
49 *That I know* ed. (*ends l. 48 in 1602*)
51 *framed* made, created

I do not cry; ask Pedro, and ask Jaques;
Not I indeed, we are very merry, very merry.
ISABELLA
  How? be merry here, be merry here?
  Is not this the place, and this the very tree,   60
  Where my Horatio died, where he was murdered?
HIERONIMO
  Was – do not say what: let her weep it out.
  This was the tree, I set it of a kernel,
  And when our hot Spain could not let it grow,
  But that the infant and the human sap   65
  Began to wither, duly twice a morning
  Would I be sprinkling it with fountain water.
  At last it grew, and grew, and bore and bore,
  Till at length
  It grew a gallows, and did bear our son.   70
  It bore thy fruit and mine: O wicked, wicked plant.
                One knocks within at the door
  See who knock there.
PEDRO   It is a painter, sir.
HIERONIMO
  Bid him come in, and paint some comfort,
  For surely there's none lives but painted comfort.
  Let him come in. One knows not what may chance: 75
  God's will that I should set this tree – but even so
  Masters ungrateful servants rear from naught,
  And then they hate them that did bring them up.

Enter the PAINTER

PAINTER
  God bless you, sir.
HIERONIMO
  Wherefore? why, thou scornful villain,   80
  How, where, or by what means should I be blessed?

61 *died* ed. (hied *1602*)
64 ff. *our hot Spain* a much stronger sense of actual locality than in Kyd's text
69 *Till . . . length* ed. (*begins l. 70 in 1602*)
74 *painted* false, merely apparent
76 *but even so* ed. (*begins l. 77 in 1602*)
76–7 The dash in l. 76 represents the anguished question implied in the preceding
    phrase: 'Can it also be God's will that it should grow to such terrible uses?
80 *Wherefore?* Why?

ISABELLA

What wouldst thou have, good fellow?

PAINTER   Justice, madam.

HIERONIMO

O ambitious beggar, wouldst thou have that
That lives not in the world?
Why, all the undelved mines cannot buy   85
An ounce of justice, 'tis a jewel so inestimable:
I tell thee,
God hath engrossed all justice in his hands,
And there is none, but what comes from him.

PAINTER

O then I see   90
That God must right me for my murdered son.

HIERONIMO

How, was thy son murdered?

PAINTER

Ay sir, no man did hold a son so dear.

HIERONIMO

What, not as thine? that's a lie
As massy as the earth: I had a son,   95
Whose least unvalued hair did weigh
A thousand of thy sons: and he was murdered.

PAINTER

Alas sir, I had no more but he.

HIERONIMO

Nor I, nor I: but this same one of mine
Was worth a legion: but all is one.   100
Pedro, Jaques, go in a-doors: Isabella go,
And this good fellow here and I
Will range this hideous orchard up and down,
Like to two lions reaved of their young.
Go in a-doors, I say.   105

                    Exeunt [ISABELLA, PEDRO, JAQUES]
                    The PAINTER *and he sits down*

85 *undelved* unworked
87 *I tell thee* ed. (*begins l. 88 in 1602*)
88 *engrossed* taken up
90–4 The writer of this Addition develops Kyd's device of including a surrogate
       for Hieronimo, 'The lively portrait of my dying self' (III, xiii, 85).
90 *O then I see* ed. (*begins l. 91 in 1602*)
95 *massy* huge, weighty
100 *all is one* no matter
103 *range* walk up and down
104 *reaved* bereft, robbed

Come, let's talk wisely now. Was thy son murdered?

PAINTER

Ay sir.

HIERONIMO

So was mine. How dost take it? Art thou not sometimes
mad? Is there no tricks that comes before thine eyes?

PAINTER

O Lord, yes sir.   110

HIERONIMO

Art a painter? Canst paint me a tear, or a wound, a groan, or
a sigh? Canst paint me such a tree as this?

PAINTER

Sir, I am sure you have heard of my painting, my name's
Bazardo.

HIERONIMO

Bazardo! afore God, an excellent fellow! Look you sir, do   115
you see, I'd have you paint me in my gallery, in your oil
colours matted, and draw me five years younger than I am.
Do you see sir, let five years go, let them go, like the
marshal of Spain. My wife Isabella standing by me, with a
speaking look to my son Horatio, which should intend to   120
this or some such like purpose: 'God bless thee, my sweet
son': and my hand leaning upon his head, thus, sir, do you
see? may it be done?

PAINTER

Very well sir.

HIERONIMO

Nay, I pray mark me sir. Then sir, would I have you paint   125
me this tree, this very tree. Canst paint a doleful cry?

PAINTER

Seemingly, sir.

HIERONIMO

Nay, it should cry: but all is one. Well sir, paint me a youth
run through and through with villains' swords, hanging
upon this tree. Canst thou draw a murderer?   130

---

116 *me in my* ed. (me my *1602*)

117 *matted* Perhaps 'made dull or matt'; but Boas may be right in suggesting 'set in a
mat or mount'.

119–23 These and the following lines are used by Hattaway (p. 105) as a basis for
inferring that 'we have to do with a species of pageant play, a parade of great
theatrical emblems calling for bold gestic acting'.

120 *speaking* eloquent, full of meaning

120 *intend to* signify

127 *Seemingly* in illusion

PAINTER

I'll warrant you sir, I have the pattern of the most notorious
villains that ever lived in all Spain.

HIERONIMO

O, let them be worse, worse: stretch thine art, and let their
beards be of Judas his own colour, and let their eyebrows
jutty over: in any case observe that. Then sir, after some   135
violent noise, bring me forth in my shirt, and my gown
under mine arm, with my torch in my hand, and my sword
reared up thus: and with these words:

What noise is this? who calls Hieronimo?
May it be done?   140

PAINTER

Yea sir.

HIERONIMO

Well sir, then bring me forth, bring me through alley and
alley, still with a distracted countenance going along, and
let my hair heave up my night-cap. Let the clouds scowl,
make the moon dark, the stars extinct, the winds blowing,   145
the bells tolling, the owl shrieking, the toads croaking, the
minutes jarring, and the clock striking twelve. And then at
last, sir, starting, behold a man hanging: and tottering, and
tottering as you know the wind will weave a man, and I
with a trice to cut him down. And looking upon him by the   150
advantage of my torch, find it to be my son Horatio. There
you may show a passion, there you may show a passion.
Draw me like old Priam of Troy, crying 'The house is a-
fire, the house is a-fire as the torch over my head!' Make me
curse, make me rave, make me cry, make me mad, make me   155
well again, make me curse hell, invocate heaven, and in the
end leave me in a trance; and so forth.

131 *pattern* model, portrait
134 *Judas ... colour* red (Judas Iscariot was alleged to be red-haired)
135 *jutty* project
135-9 These lines may provide us with a good indication of Elizabethan practice in
      staging the first lines of II, v in the main play.
142 s.p. HIERONIMO ed. (*not in 1602*)
147 *jarring* ed. (iering *1602*) ticking away
148 *tottering* dangling, swinging to and fro
149 *weave* weave about, make him swing (*O.E.D.* does not give this transitive sense)
150 *with a trice* instantly
151 *advantage* assistance
152 *show* ed. (*not in 1602*)
153-7 The closeness of these lines to the First Player's speech (*Hamlet* II, ii) is
      intriguing.

PAINTER

And is this the end?

HIERONIMO

O no, there is no end: the end is death and madness! As I
am never better than when I am mad, then methinks I am a   160
brave fellow, then I do wonders: but reason abuseth me,
and there's the torment, there's the hell. At the last, sir,
bring me to one of the murderers, were he as strong as
Hector, thus would I tear and drag him up and down.

He beats the PAINTER *in, then comes out again with a book in
his hand*

Fifth Addition, replacing IV, iv, 168 to 190 (pp. 119–20)

[CASTILE

Why hast thou butchered both my children thus?]

HIERONIMO

But are you sure they are dead?

CASTILE   Ay, slave, too sure.

HIERONIMO

What, and yours too?

VICEROY

Ay, all are dead, not one of them survive.

HIERONIMO

Nay then, I care not, come, and we shall be friends:
Let us lay our heads together;   5
See here's a goodly noose will hold them all.

VICEROY

O damned devil, how secure he is.

HIERONIMO

Secure, why dost thou wonder at it?
I tell thee Viceroy, this day I have seen revenge,
And in that sight am grown a prouder monarch   10
Than ever sat under the crown of Spain:
Had I as many lives as there be stars,
As many heavens to go to as those lives,
I'd give them all, ay, and my soul to boot,

159 Hamilton associates this line with Hieronimo's repeated attempts to discern or
    create an order in experience, and his repeated disappointment.
161 *brave* glorious, splendid   161 *abuseth* deceives
  7 *secure* confident   9 *revenge* ed. (reueng'd *1602*)
 14 *to boot* in addition

But I would see thee ride in this red pool.   15
CASTILE
Speak, who were thy confederates in this?
VICEROY
That was thy daughter Bel-imperia,
For by her hand my Balthazar was slain:
I saw her stab him.
HIERONIMO   Oh, good words:
As dear to me was my Horatio,   20
As yours, or yours, or yours, my lord, to you.
My guiltless son was by Lorenzo slain,
And by Lorenzo, and that Balthazar,
Am I at last revenged thoroughly,
Upon whose souls may heavens be yet revenged   25
With greater far than these afflictions.
Methinks since I grew inward with revenge,
I cannot look with scorn enough on death.
KING
What, dost thou mock us, slave? Bring tortures forth.
HIERONIMO
Do, do, do, and meantime I'll torture you.   30
You had a son, as I take it: and your son
Should ha' been married to your daughter:
Ha, was't not so? You had a son too,
He was my liege's nephew. He was proud,
And politic. Had he lived, he might ha' come   35
To wear the crown of Spain, I think 'twas so:
'Twas I that killed him; look you, this same hand,
'Twas it that stabbed his heart; do you see, this hand?
For one Horatio, if you ever knew him, a youth,
One that they hanged up in his father's garden,   40
One that did force your valiant son to yield,
While your more valiant son did take him prisoner.
VICEROY
Be deaf my senses, I can hear no more.
KING
Fall heaven, and cover us with thy sad ruins.

19 *Oh, good words:* ed. (*begins l. 20 in 1602*)
27 ~~inward with~~ closely acquainted with
29 *tortures* instruments of torture
31–3 Hieronimo speaks first to the viceroy and then ('your daughter') to Castile.
    The son (l. 33) is Lorenzo.
35 *ha'* ed. (a *1602*)

CASTILE
  Roll all the world within thy pitchy cloud.   45
HIERONIMO
  Now do I applaud what I have acted
          Nunc iners cadat manus.
  Now to express the rupture of my part,
  [First take my tongue, and afterwards my heart.]

END

47 *iners cadat* ed. (*mers cadae 1602*) 'Now let my hand fall idle'.
48 *the . . . part* the breaking-off of my role